S0-EIA-760

THE EAGER IMMIGRANTS

A Survey of the
Life and Americanization of
Jewish immigrants to the United States

by

David M. Zielonka
Rabbi, Temple Emanuel
Gastonia, North Carolina
Lecturer, Gaston College
Dallas, North Carolina

and

Robert J. Wechman, Ph.D.
BMCC, City University of New York
St. Thomas Aquinas College
Pace University

2nd Printing

Copyright 1972
Stipes Publishing Co.
ISBN-0-87563-044-8

Published By
STIPES PUBLISHING COMPANY
10-12 Chester Street
Champaign, Illinois

Dedication

To Our Parents

PREFACE

Americanization is a difficult term to define. It includes, to be sure, the adoption by the immigrant of American language, clothing, personal and national goals, life style, loyalties, interests and attitudes - - all of which have been and are constantly in flux. But it also includes the willingness of "native Americans," who were themselves often already-Americanized immigrants or the children of immigrants, to accept the newcomers and allow them to become part of the American scene. This factor, too, has been tempered by a multiplicity of social, economic and political variables; and it has varied from "The Golden Door" to total exclusionism.

Definition of the terms *Jew, Jewish* and *Judaism* is equally difficult. The Jewish religious culture brought to America by Jewish immigrants varied from devoutly orthodox to radically reform, from those to whom Judaism was a total way of life to those for whom religion was merely an appendage to existence, from those who were determined to re-establish old-world Jewish life in America to those whose efforts were directed to becoming un-Jewish as quickly as possible.

The following is an attempt to survey the interaction of these two variables in the 300-plus years of American Jewish communal life. The European and American setting for each epoch is included because Jewish history is not a self-contained study; it unfolds only in the world of time and events, of which it is often a microcosm. Rather than attempting to enumerate every happening in every city, representative samplings have been chosen to show the trends, moods and patterns of the Americanizing process which transformed successive waves of Jewish Immigrants into continuing generations of successful, enthusiastic Americans. Chapter divisions are based on the periodization first suggested in Peter Wiernik's *History of the Jews in America,* (1912) and developed in Jacob Rader Marcus' "The Periodization of American Jewish History" (published in *Studies in American Jewish History, 1969).*

i

TABLE OF CONTENTS

PREFACE i
THE SEPHARDIC PERIOD............................ 1
   In the Colonies 2
   New Amsterdam-1654-1664 2
   In the British Colonies 5
   In the New Nation 7
   Notes for the Sephardic Period 11
THE GERMAN PERIOD 13
   Background 14
   Immigration Statistics 17
   Nature of the Immigrants 17
   Government Actions 20
   Organizations 23
   Economic Life............................. 26
   The War Between the States 28
   Social Integration and Anti-Semitism............ 30
   Education 31
   The Reform Movement 33
   The Traditionalists......................... 38
   Notes on the German Period 40
THE EAST EUROPEAN PERIOD..................... 45
   Jews in Russia-Background..................... 46
   Immigration Statistics 49
   The New Immigrants-General Nature 50
   Efforts to Aid the Immigrants 52
   Agricultural Colonies......................... 55
   Economics-Introduction 55
   The Needle Trades and the Jewish Labor
      Movement 56
   Journalism 59
   The Yiddish Theatre 61
   Education-Introduction 62
   Classes for the Children 63
   Programs for the Adults...................... 66
   Synagogues 67
   Notes for the East European Period 69
THE AMERICAN PERIOD 73
   The End of Immigration....................... 74
   Immigration Statistics 75
   Anti-Semitism 76
   Cultural Pluralism 79
   Notes on the American Period 85
BIBLIOGRAPHY.................................. 87
INDEX... 93

THE SEPHARDIC PERIOD

In the Colonies

The history of Jewish immigration to America begins indirectly with the marriage of Ferdinand of Aragon and Isabella of Castille. From this union, through which a united Christian Spain was formed, came the impetus for the formation of the Inquisition and ultimately the expulsion of Jews from Spain and, later, Portugal. Among the many places in which the Jewish exiles took refuge were the newly discovered and settled islands of the Americas. By the seventeenth century there were Jewish settlements in almost all the trading outposts of the New World. In the Spanish and Portuguese colonies the Inquisition wielded great power. In British and French settlements Jews were allowed more freedom but had few legal rights. It was in the Dutch possessions in Brazil and the Indies that Jews enjoyed the greatest liberty. From 1630 to 1654 the Jewish community of Recife, on the Brazilian coast, had a synagogue and Jewish communal organizations. In 1654, while the Dutch and English were diverted by Cromwell's mercantile war (1652-1654), the Portuguese recaptured Recife.

New Amsterdam — 1654 - 1664

When Portugal took over Recife, the life of its thriving and prosperous Jewish community came to an abrupt end. Some five thousand Jewish settlers left Recife to escape the terror of the Inquisition. Many followed Moses Aguilar and Isaac Aboab back to Holland; others sought refuge in Surinam, Curacao, Jamaica, Barbados, Guadaloupe and Martinique; and one small group found their way to New Amsterdam.

The twenty three who arrived on the St. Charles were not the first Jews known in the North American colonies. An Elias Legardo, who was probably a Jew, is noted in Virginia in 1621; [1] in 1649 a Solomon Franco was "warned out" of Massachusetts; [2] and Jacob Barsimson was already in New Amsterdam when the fateful shipload arrived in 1654. [3]

This group is important, however, because it contained the first Jewish families who settled and formed a distinct community on American soil.

Life for these new colonists was difficult. Peter Stuyvesant, the governor of New Netherland, was hostile to all who dissented from the dominant Dutch Reformed Church. He immediately wrote to the directors of the Dutch West India Company in Amsterdam for permission to expel these members of the "deceitful race," [4] to insure that "none of the Jewish nation be permitted to infest New Netherland." [5]

The directors' reply, dated April 26, 1655, began with the ominous words:

2

> We would have liked to effectuate and fulfill your wishes and request, that the new territories should no more be allowed to be infected by the people of the Jewish nation, for we foresee therefrom the same difficulties which you fear.

The letter, concluded, however, with the decision that such a policy

> would be unreasonable and unfair, especially because of the considerable loss sustained by this nation, with others, in the taking of Brazil, and also because of the large amount of capital which they still have invested in the shares of this company. Therefore, after may deliberations we have decided and resolved to apostille [order, written as a marginal note] upon a certain petition made by said Portuguese Jews, that these people may travel and trade to and in New Netherland and live and remain there, provided the poor among them shall not become a burden to the company or the community, but be supported by their own nation.[6]

Stuyvesant and the Council were careful not to grant to their new fellow-colonists any privileges not already held by the Jews of Amsterdam. The Jews could stay, but they could not engage in retail trade, practice any craft, hold public office, serve in the trainbands, or practice their religion in a synagogue or public gathering. Worship services and holy day observances, when held, were conducted in private homes.

It may have been that Stuyvesant, overruled in his attempt to drive the Jews away, was trying an alternative course - - to make staying in New Netherland less appealing than removing to Holland or one of the other Dutch colonies. Not only was New Amsterdam an isolated trading outpost, but every right, even those specifically granted by the Dutch West India Company was realized only after a struggle. Those who chose to leave found, in all likelihood, a better and easier life; but a certain number chose to remain despite the difficulties.[7] In spite of the governor's opposition, the Jewish community soon established itself.

The Directors of the Dutch West India Company wrote to Stuyvesant on June 14, 1656:

> We have seen and heard with displeasure, that your Honors, against our apostille of the 15th of February, 1655, granted to the Jewish or Portuguese nation at their request, you have forbidden them to trade at Fort Orange [Albany] and South [Delaware] River, and also the purchase of real estate, which is allowed them here in this country [Holland] without difficulty, and we wish that this had not occurred but that your Honors had obeyed your orders which you must hereafter execute punctually and with

more respect. Jews or Portuguese people, however, shall not be permitted to establish themselves as mechanics (which they are not allowed to do in this city [Amsterdam]) nor allowed to have open retail shops, but they may quietly and peacefully carry on their business as heretofore and exercise in all quietness their religion within their houses, for which end they must without doubt endeavor to build their houses close together in a convenient place on one or the other side of New Amsterdam - - at their choice - - as they have done here.[8]

On August 28, 1655, a regulation was approved that Jews be exempt from service in the Burgher Guard, and that in place of service in the Guard they pay a special monthly tax. In November of that year, Jacob Barsimson and Asser Levy petitioned the Council for permission to serve in the Guard or, at least, to be relieved of the additional tax, which they were too poor to pay. The Council dismissed their petition with the added remark that "since the petitioners are of the opinion that the result of this will be injurious to them, consent is hereby given to them to depart whenever and whither it pleases them."[9] Shortly, however the ruling was changed; and Barsimson and Levy were allowed to keep "watch and ward."

In July, 1656, land was allotted for a Jewish burial ground. This was, as it would later be in many cities, the first permanent Jewish communal institution.

A year later, on April 11, 1657, Levy petitioned for burgher rights and a burgher certificate (which could have been his by right in Amsterdam). When his request was rejected, an appeal was addressed "To the Noble Worships, the Director General and Council of New Netherland." Citing an earlier ruling of the directors in Amsterdam, they asked that the Council

please not exclude nor shut us off from the burgher right, but to notify the Noble Burgomasters that they should permit us, like other burghers, to enjoy the burgher right, and for this purpose to give the customary burgher certificate.

Without waiting for orders from Amsterdam, Stuyvesant and the Council approved the Petition.[10]

During the remaining years of Dutch rule, little else changed for the Jewish community. Although a discernable community remained, many of the original settlers left for Holland or the Dutch possessions in the Americas, where they could enjoy considerably more freedom; and although some new settlers came to the New Netherland, the Jewish community probably numbered no more than 300 when the British took over the colony and renamed it New York.

In the British Colonies

Jews in the British colonies lived primarily in east coast port cities: Newport, New York, Philadelphia, Charleston (then called Charles Town) and Savannah. The Jewish communal life of these settlers centered on the synagogues which were founded as soon as there were enough Jews to support a congregation. These synagogues followed the Sephardic (Spanish and Portuguese) liturgy, which came to be regarded as "the American custom." The founders and leaders of the congregations were generally Spanish or Portuguese in origin, although many, and in some cases a majority of the membership and of the more affluent members were of Ashkenazic (French, German or East European) origin. Similar to its status in Europe, but with considerably less authority, the synagogue served as the religious, social and philanthropic center; and its leaders served as spokesman for the entire Jewish community. None of the congregations was served by an ordained rabbi (the first ordained rabbi to serve an American congregation on a permanent basis did not come until 1840). Professional leadership for the congregations, when it was available, came from cantors who were engaged to serve in the combined role of teacher, worship leader, preacher and "minister." Traveling rabbis, usually fund raising emissaries from the schools and communities of Palestine, did occasionally come to the colonies, but their visits were usually quite brief and none remained. The most famous of these *m'shullachim* was Rabbi Haim Isaac Carigal, whose sermon delivered on Shavuot (Pentecost) in 1773 was the first Jewish sermon published in America.[11] Carigal became a friend and frequent correspondent of Reverend Ezra Stiles, later president of Yale.

Jews in the colonies were for the most part merchants, mercantile traders and artisans. Most came voluntarily, seeking commercial opportunities which the new colonies offered; some came to escape religious persecution; and a few came as indentured servants. In general their relations with non-Jews were cordial. "These colonial Jews found American society so congenial that they rapidly abandoned clothing and habits that set them apart from Christian society. Most of them shaved regularly, ate pork and took their religion lightly."[12] A study of the wills left by Jews in 18th century New York shows a wide variety of both Jewish and communal interests. In true American Colonial style, many of these wills begin, "In the Name of God, Amen" - - a formula not usually found in the Jewish religious tradition.[13]

The leading Jewish community in colonial America was Newport, Rhode Island. The first Jewish settlement in Newport was recorded in 1658, and in the same year Congregation Jeshuat Israel was founded.[14] Newport was a major trading port with the

West Indies, and its Jewish community consisted mainly of merchants. Jews had commercial and religious rights, but not political rights. "In 1763, Jews were denied the right to vote and other rights of citizenship in the colonies and even in what is supposedly the cradle of freedom, the colony of Rhode Island."[15] The American candle-making industry, which centered in Newport, was developed by Jacob Rodrigues Rivera, a Portuguese Jew who introduced the technique of manufacturing sperm-whale oil, and his son-in-law, Aaron Lopez, who organized the spermaceti candle-making industry and founded the first American candle-makers guild. Isaac Touro, an outspoken patriot and revolutionary, served as "minister" of the congregation until the British invaded and destroyed Newport during the Revolution.

The Jews of New York at first enjoyed the same freedom under the British which they had known under the Dutch, and gradually attained almost complete freedom. Restrictive laws against Jews were generally not enforced. A Swedish visitor to America, Peter Kalm, speaking of the Jews of New York in 1748, said: "They enjoy all the privileges common to other inhabitants of this town and province."[16] The first permanent synagogue was established by 1695; in 1728 it was reorganized and was named Shearith Israel. A well known "minister" of the congregation was Gershom Mendes Seixas. Seixas' strong American nationalist sermons so antagonized the British that he was forced to flee New York City, and he spent most of the Revolutionary years in Philadelphia. Another New Yorker, Hayman Levy, at one time employed John Jacob Astor at the rate of a dollar a day beating the pelts brought in by his Indian trading.

The first permanent Jewish settlement in Philadelphia was recorded about 1703, and the community grew very slowly until the time of the Revolution. Congregation Mikveh Israel was founded about 1745 and included in its membership the Gratz, Franks and Levy families, who were leading colonial merchants and among the original signers of the non-importation agreements. Merchants from Philadelphia founded Jewish communities in Lancaster and Easton, Pennsylvania, and ventured as far north as Canada to establish trading outposts.

The constitution of South Carolina, drawn up by political philosopher John Locke in 1669, guaranteed complete freedom of religion to all groups believing in a Supreme Being. The Jewish community of Charleston was small and was able to organize a congregation only in 1750, after its numbers were supplemented by Jewish merchants and landowners from Georgia who were escaping the slave insurrections of the 1740's. Among the community were the leading American indigo growers, Moses Lindo and Francis Salvador, who was a member of the Provincial Congress of South Carolina in 1775 and was killed during one of the early battles of the American Revolution.

The Jewish community of Savannah was founded in 1733, only a month after the colony was chartered by General James Oglethorpe. A year later its congregation, Mickve Israel, was founded. Members of the Jewish community of Georgia were merchants, landowners and cattle breeders. Abraham deLyon, a Portuguese Jew, introduced viniculture and silk production to Georgia. John Wesley, the founder of Methodism, learned Spanish during the time he lived in Georgia "in order to converse with my Jewish parishoners, some whom seem nearer the mind of Christ than many of those who call him Lord."

Jews were scattered throughout all the colonies and in Canada in pursuit of trade. In most places there were not enough of them to form a congregation and insure permanent settlement. Jews were generally accepted and allowed to become active in the everyday life of the colonies. (One notable exception was the colony of Maryland, where Dr. Jacob Lumbrozo was tried in 1658 for the capital crime of blasphemy because he was not a Trinitarian Christian.) In spite of the freedom and the ease of economic and social advancement which the colonies provided, the colonial Jewish community grew very slowly. In the years from 1664 to 1776 the Colonial Jewish community grew only from approximately 300 to about 2,500 inhabitants. This was one-tenth of the growth rate of the colonies at large.[17]

In The New Nation

When the Revolutionary War broke out, the small Jewish community in the colonies realized that its vital interests were at stake. Colonial Jews were mostly townspeople - - traders, peddlers, merchant shippers, artisans, and tradesmen - - and they opposed the British mercantile policy which strictly controlled commerce. In addition, Jews realized that they were more free in America than anywhere else in the world, and they believed that if the American Revolution was successful, these freedoms would be guaranteed.

Jews were active in many phases of the War. Some served in the military, others were army sutlers or purveyors, some dealt in international trade (by smuggling, when the British blockade encouraged such action) and by raising money to finance the Revolution. The most successful financier was Haym Salomon, a Polish Jew, who was unusally successful in the marketing of American letters of credit.

The American Jewish community was the unforeseen beneficiary of the colonial alliance against England. Because of the religious diversity among the various colonies, their alliance was founded on commercial and secular-national ideals. To avoid religious controversy, church and state were separated in law and policy. This secular union of American States has continued and is a primary reason for the general lack of religious conflict in the United States.

In the era of the American Revolution, the Jew was well accepted as a part of the life of Rhode Island, New York, Pennsylvania, Virginia, South Carolina and Georgia. In the other states, the combination of legal restrictions and the lack of commercial opportunities minimized Jewish settlement and assimilation. In every area where they settled, the Jews quickly absorbed colonial culture and, except in religion, were indistinguishable from the rest of the populace.

The new nation in the post war period was beset with many problems. The newly independent states adopted protectionist tariffs against one another, and the national government was unable to do anything to prevent this. Settlement of the northwest opened up new trade routes, and gave increased opportunity for land speculation. Many banks, insurance companies, shippers and land speculators incorporated, and there was much speculation in stocks, securities and loan certificates. Jews were active participants in these business ventures. In Philadelphia there were at least seven Jewish broker-bankers; and Moses Seixas was cashier of the Bank of Rhode Island. Jacob I. Cohen and Isaiah Isaacs, owners of the largest Jewish mercantile company in Richmond, Virginia, purchased a tract of land on the Licking River in Kentucky. The man hired to survey their tract of land was Daniel Boone.[18]

The United States Constitution guaranteed the freedom of the American Jewish community. The principle of the separation of Church and State was maintained in the Constitution. Article VI of the Constitution stated that "no religious test shall ever be required as a qualification to any office or public trust under the United States," and Amendment I provided that "Congress shall make no law respecting an establishment of religion, or prohibiting the free exercise thereof." In addition, acts such, as the Northwest Ordiance of 1787, which established full political and religious freedom, and the removal of religious barriers by the various states served as further encouragement for Jews to settle in the United States. The Constitutions of the states, many of which had not incorporated these principles prior to their ratification of the Constitution, subsequently came to include them.

In addition to these legal enactments, the actions of government leaders also reflected an attitude of religious freedom. In 1788, Benjamin Franklin was one of the contributors to the building fund of Congregation Mikveh Israel of Philadelphia. In 1789, at the festivities in Philadelphia celebrating the new Constitution, one of the refreshment tables was supplied with food that conformed to Jewish dietary laws. Despite the small number of Jews in the city, Jewish sensibilities were taken into consideration.[19] Further encouragement was given to the Jews by George Washington's letter to the Hebrew Congregation in Newport, Rhode Island, in 1790:

> It is now no more that toleration is spoken of as if it were the indulgence of one class of people that another enjoyed the exercise of their inherent natural rights, for happily, the Government of the United States, which gives to bigotry no sanction, to persecution no assistance, requires only that they who live under its protection should demean themselves as good citizens in giving it on all occasions their effectual support.

The President continued:

> May the children of the stock of Abraham who dwell in this land continue to merit and enjoy the good will of the other inhabitants; while every one shall sit in safety under his own vine and fig trees and there shall be none to make him afraid.
>
> May the father of all mercies scatter light, and not darkness, upon our paths, and make us all in our several vocations useful here, and in His own due time and way everlastingly happy.[20]

Letters expressing the same sentiments were also sent to the Jewish communities of Philadelphia and Savannah. Acts such as these suggested that the Jews living in the United States were full participants in the life of the nation as neighbors, business associates and friends.

From 1789 to 1812 the American Jewish community stayed about the same size. Travel was made difficult by European Wars, and the number of immigrants was small. Losses to the Jewish community from intermarriage, conversion and emigration at least offset any natural increase or immigration. The new states of Vermont, Kentucky and Tennessee had almost no Jews, nor were there many in the territory acquired by the Louisiana Purchase.

The most colorful and influential Jewish figure of this period was Mordecai Manuel Noah. Having served in the War of 1812, his later career included journalism (at one time he owned several New York newspapers), play writing (one of his plays ran in London and New York in 1820) and pioneering (he attempted unsuccessfully to found an American Zion on Grand Island in the Niagara River). Most significant was his political career, which showed the degree in which Jews had become accepted in America. In 1813, Noah was appointed American Consul to Tunis by President James Madison, a post which he held for three years. After his return he served as High Sheriff of New York City, was later appointed Surveyor of the Port of New York by President

Jackson, and in 1841 served as Associate Judge of the New York Court of Sessions.[21]

In the first half of the 19th century, Jews lived throughout the United States and had adopted the life-style of their respective regions. Many Jews living in the South adopted the genteel manners and the code of honor associated with Southern gentlemen. "Henry Stanley, the future explorer of Africa, encountered this powerful social force while clerking in a country store in Arkansas. In Cypress Bend he was amazed to see his fellow clerks and the plain farmers who visited the store bowing to a stern code of conduct that was aristocratic in origin - - the obligation to uphold personal honor. Even the proprietor of the store, a German Jew, quickly resented any suggestion of insult and used a dueling pistol."[22]

From 1815 to 1840 Jewish immigration to the United States increased, but it was not comparable to the numbers that entered the country after 1840. During this period, the American Jewish community increased from 3,000 to 15,000 inhabitants. Most of these immigrants came from Central Europe, remained in America's east coast cities, and laid the groundwork for the substantial German-Jewish immigration which followed after 1840.

FOOTNOTES

For the Sephardic Period

1.   Joseph L. Blau and Salo W. Baron, ed. *The Jews of the United States, 1790-1840: A Documentary History* (New York: Columbia University Press, and Philadelphia: The Jewish Publication Society of America, 1963), Vol. I, p. xvii. Also: Anita Libman Lebeson, "The American Jewish Chronicle," in Louis Finkelstein, ed., *The Jews: Their History, Culture and Religion,* 3rd. edn. (Philadelphia: The Jewish Publication Society of America, 1960), Vol. I, p. 451.

2.   Leon Huhner, "The Jews of New England (Other than Rhode Island) Prior to 1800," in *Publications of the American Jewish Historical Society* (Baltimore: Lord Baltimore Press of the Friedenwald Company, 1903), Vol. XI, p. 78.

3.   Jacob Rader Marcus, *Early American Jewry* (Philadelphia: The Jewish Publication Society of America, 1951), Vol. I, p. 24.

4.   Rufus Learsi, *The Jews in America: A History* (Cleveland and New York: The World Publishing Co., 1954), p. 26.

5.   Peter Wiernik, *History of the Jews in America* (New York, The Jewish Press Publishing Company, 1912), p. 63

6.   Morris U. Schappes, *A Documentary History of the Jews of the United States, 1654-1875,* rev. ed. (New York: The Citadel Press, 1952), pp. 4-5.

7.   See: Marcus, pp. 32-33; see also Miriam K. Freund, *Jewish Merchants in Colonial America* (New York: Behrman's Jewish Book House, 1939), pp. 21-43

8.   Schappes, pp. 11-12.

9.   *Ibid.,* p. 6.

10.   Marcus, pp. 30-33

11.   This was reprinted under the title "Rabbi Carigal Preaches in Newport" by the American Jewish Archives, Cincinnati (1966).

12.   Nathaniel Weyl, *The Jew in American Politics* (New Rochelle, New York: Arlington House, 1968), p. 35.

13.   Leo Hershkowitz, *Wills of Early New York Jews (1704-1799)* (New York: The American Jewish Historical Society, 1967), p. viii, Studies in American Jewish History, No. 4.

14.   The Sephardic congregations founded during this period were generally given names with messianic overtones. For example, Jeshuat Israel Means "the salvation of Israel": Shearith Israel (New York) means "the remnant of Israel"; and Mikveh Israel (Philadelphia and Savannah) means "the hope of Israel."

15.   *Lawrence Henry Gipson, The Coming of the Revolution* (New York: Harper Torchbooks, 1962), p. 13.

16.   Blau and Baron, II, xxi.

17.   For detailed studies of life in Colonial America see: Marcus, *Early American Jewry,* Vols. I and II; Bertram W. Korn, *Jews and Negro Slavery in the Old South* (Elkins Park, Pa.: Reform Congregational Keneseth Israel, 1961); Lee M. Friedman, *Early American Jews* (Cambridge, Mass.: Harvard University Press, 1934); Freund, *Jewish Merchants in Colonial America.* For detailed studies of individual communities see: Hyman B. Grinstein, *The Rise of the Jewish Community of New York, 1654-1860* (Philadelphia: The Jewish Publication Society of America, 1954); Edwin Wolf, 2nd, and Maxwell Whiteman, *The History of the Jews of Philadelphia from Colonial Times to the Age of Jackson* (Philadelphia: The Jewish Publication Society of America, 1957); Charles Reznikoff and Uriah Z. Engelman, *The Jews of Charleston* (Philadelphia: The Jewish Publication Society of America, 1950).

18.   Jacob Rader Marcus, *American Jewry: Documents, Eighteenth Century* (Cincinnati: The Hebrew Union College Press, 1959), pp. 441-449.

19.   Blau and Baron, I, xxiii.

20.   *Ibid.,* pp. 9-10.

21.   For a more complete biography see: *The Jewish Encyclopedia* (New York: Funk & Wagnalls Co., 1905), Vol. IX, pp. 323-324.

22.   Clement Eaton, *The Growth of Southern Civilization* (New York: Harper Torchbooks, 1963), p. 2.

THE GERMAN PERIOD

Background

The German Jew of the late eighteenth century had begun to make his way out of the ghetto. The desire to build a unified state with a sound economy, combined with the influence of Enlightenment ideas, led to the liberation of certain segments of the Jewish community. As early as the 1770's Moses Mendelssohn[1] was one of the favorites of salon society and a leading German philosopher and literary critic. Because of the life he led as a *Schutzjud* (protected Jew), he was able to contrast German society with that in the German-Jewish ghetto of his childhood. Many of his efforts were directed toward preparing other Jews for life outside the ghetto.

To teach the German language to ghetto dwellers, he made a translation of the Five Books of Moses into German, spelling the words phonetically in Hebrew characters. Later he prepared a commentary in Hebrew on these books. With several colleagues Mendelssohn published the Hebrew language magazine *Ha-M'asef (The Gatherer)*, which featured articles on German culture and philosophy. Supported by his wealthy German friends, he sponsored a school for Jewish children in which the German language and occupational training were taught in addition to traditional Jewish subjects.

Because Mendelssohn was popular, well known and admired, he was able to implement his ideas, and his hopes were partially realized. Gotthold Ephraim Lessing, a Christian German dramatist, wrote *Nathan the Wise* in 1779, in which he contended that no religion had a monopoly on truth and the Christian could only justify his faith by treating the Jews properly. Because of Lessing's influence, a greater tolerance towards Jews was manifested.[2]

As a consequence of the French Revolution and the victories of Napoleon Bonaparte, a period of emancipation arrived for the European Jews. The Jews, now treated as citizens, believed that they must become more familiar with the culture and customs of the various European countries and must show themselves to be worthy citizens, keeping themselves above reproach in the eyes of their gentile countrymen.[3] This drive toward cultural assimilation, which was different from religious assimilation and was not intended to include it, was later manifested in the United States.

In the three years between the creation of the Supreme Council of Israelites (January, 1809) and the edict granting Jews equal rights as citizens (1812), Jews in all the newly created departments and confederations of the French Empire were granted greatly increased freedom.[4] As the Jews were gradually freed from the confines of the ghetto, they were exposed more and more to various non-Jewish experiences. As the opportunities for Jews grew and their horizons expanded, they wished to become more active participants in the civilization of Enlightened Germany. To a limited degree, they succeeded during the years of Napolean's rule.

Most of the liberties which were granted to European Jews by Napoleonic France were rescinded after the Congress of Vienna in 1815. Despite the efforts of leading members of the Vienna Jewish community and the representations made to the Congress by delegations of Jewish communities throughout Germany, the trend of the Congress was toward restoring Europe to its position prior to Napoleon. Many of the Napoleonic innovations were reversed; one of these was the emancipation of European Jews. Except in France, where legal disabilities were gradually removed, Jews were quickly returned to the legal status they held prior to Napoleon.[5]

After 1815 a period of reaction set in. In the Kingdom of Vienna, the Hapsburg domains, the Papal states, and the Bourbon lands in Naples and Sicily, all Napoleonic reforms were dropped. Jews living in these lands were deprived of equality before the law, religious toleration, political rights and personal freedom; and they were legally powerless even to protest this restoration of medievalism. Only in the areas of Tuscany and Lombardy-Venetia were Jews given any rights at all (though they still could not hold public office, own real estate or practice a profession). In the Papal States, under the rule of Pius VII and Leo XII the Inquisition was restored; ghettos were re-instituted; Jews were required to listen to conversionist sermons and wear identifying badges; and forced conversions and the kidnapping of Jewish children were common. Because of these persecutions many Jews fled to France.

In Austria-Hungary, Prussia and Galicia old restrictions on Jews were restored. Jews could not reside in rural areas; almost every city had a *Judenstrasse* ("Jew-street"); only a few *Schutzjuden* were permitted in the major cities; police or government officials could break into Jewish homes or search individual Jews at any time for any reason; Jews were required to take a special oath before testifying in court and pay special taxes for residence and business rights.

Starting in 1816 Jews were victimized as a by-product of "Teutomania," a fanatical devotion to the ideal of a Christian German Empire, as exemplified in a highly romaticized conception of Germany during the Middle Ages. Intellectuals, politicians and churchmen competed for the privilege of hating Jews most intensely. Anti-Jewish rioting began in Wurzburg in March, 1819, following the murder of the reactionary poet and journalist August von Kotzebue by Karl Ludwig Sand, a member of the radical, anti-Semitic *Allgemeine deutsche Burschenschaft.* By August of that year, attacks on Jews became common throughout Germany. The rallying cry of the reactionary anti-Semitic groups

15

was the revived medieval "HEP, HEP!" The cities, which were legally responsible for the safety of Jews, did little to control the rioting; police and military units called in to maintain order often took part in the killing and looting. Christian clergymen often accompanied the rioters and gave them encouragement. The height of Jew-hatred came in November, 1819. Novelist Hartwig Hundt published a pamphlet, "The Mirror of the Jews," in which he advocated selling all Jews to the English for plantation slaves and killing those who would not leave. The hatred expressed in this pamphlet was so strong that it was confiscated by the state censors; and following this, overt anti-Semitism lessened for a few years.

The French Revolution of 1848 sparked the Germans into action. When news of the February Revolution in Paris reached Germany, there were simultaneous uprisings in many German cities including Berlin, the capital of Prussia. The revolt in Berlin forced Frederick William IV to grant the Berliners a constitution. The Prussian Army suppressed the revolts, but Frederick then sent the army out of Berlin because he believed that the Berliners were patriots. When the Constituent Assembly of Berlin asked for liberalized laws that would limit the power of the king, Frederick bowed to these demands and appointed a liberal ministry. In June, 1848, the Berliners revolted again and demanded free speech, schools, press, etc. The middle class, which feared social and economic revolution, demanded that Frederick assume full power again and bring the army back into Berlin. Because the middle class did not support the working class, the Revolution failed. Their actions created one of the great problems of German nationalism: the middle class, which in other western European countries supported democratic reforms, in Germany supported authoritarianism in order to maintain stability and order. The middle class' support of authoritarianism stripped Germany of a potentially democratic intellectual class that could have prevented an extremist type of nationalism from developing.

In October, 1848, representatives of the liberal democratic forces in Germany met in Frankfort, in an attempt to unite the country under a democratic constitution. The vice-president of the Assembly was Gabriel Riesser, the grandson of an Orthodox rabbi and publisher of a newspaper, *The Jew.* This assembly issued a proclamation of the fundamental rights of citizens of the German nation, similar to the French "Declaration of the Rights of Man." The Frankfort Assembly proclaimed a united Germany, and after a period of debates offered the emperorship to Frederick William IV of Prussia. He refused to accept their offer both because he detested the liberal democratic forces that made the offer and because he feared that his acceptance might draw Prussia into war with Austria. His rejection of the emperorship sounded the death knell for the liberal efforts of the Frankfort Assembly.

Because Jews were a major part of the liberal democratic element, conspicuously represented at the Frankfort Assembly and in the liberal Young Germany movement, which strongly opposed the aggressive racism of German nationalism, Jews were generally considered to be undesirable and "un-German." Because Jews had been strongly identified with the "revolutionaries" in 1848, their only alternative to further oppression was emigration. Among the political exiles following the Revolution of 1848, many were Jews.

Immigration Statistics

The exact number of Jewish immigrants prior to 1881 is impossible to ascertain. No notation of religion was made on immigration records, and the United States census did not ask the religion of respondents. Therefore, only estimates made by contemporary observers can be cited for reference.

The American Almanac estimated the American Jewish community of 1840 as 15,000. In 1848, M. A. Berk estimated a Jewish population of 50,000, including both immigrants and natural increase in his figure. William B. Hackenberg estimated the Jewish community as 230,257 in 1880, the last estimate before the keeping of accurate records began.[7]

How much of the increase was through immigration and how much of this immigration was from Germany, rather than England, France or Eastern Europe, cannot be accurately determined.

Nature of the Immigrants

German Jews had been in America since Colonial times. Some had become prominent in business, and many were active in Jewish congregational life. It is likely that by the time of the American Revolution, the majority of the American Jewish community were Ashkenazim (Jews from Central and Eastern Europe).

In political activity, the American Jews in the formative period of the new nation appear to have been Jeffersonians rather than Hamiltonians, and Democratic-Republicans rather than Federalists. This was probably due to Jefferson's favoring a low tariff, international trade and states' rights, all of which appealed to Jewish commercial interests. The American Jewish community had already changed from essentially Spanish to largely German. The Jewish immigrants from the German states were schooled in the doctrines of nineteenth century liberal thought and were attracted to the political and social doctrines of the Democratic-Republicans.[8]

In 1826, Isaac Harby, a Jewish journalist of Charleston, South Carolina, commented on Jewish immigration to the United States:

> Men, who reflect, go anywhere in pursuit of happiness. The immediate ancestors of the most respectable Jews in these United States came, some for the purposes of commerce, others for the more noble love of liberty, and the majority for both. In Georgia and in South Carolina, several honorably bore arms in the revolutionary war. My maternal grandfather contributed pecuniary aid to South Carolina, and particularly to Charleston, when besieged by the British. My father-in-law was a brave grenadier in the regular American Army, and fought and bled for the liberty he lived to enjoy, and to hand down to his children. Numerous instances of patriotism are recorded of such Israelites.
>
> As to the descent of the Jews of the United States, they are principally German and English; though South Carolina has a portion of French and Portuguese.[9]

The German Jews who immigrated during the early years of the 19th century were often well educated, comfortable with German language and culture, and more likely to associate with Germans of other religions than with Jews of other cultural traditions. Like most German immigrants of this time, they came primarily from southern Germany. While some came as families, a large part of the immigration was unmarried men, often the younger sons of poor families seeking opportunities that would not be available in Germany. Few had extensive Jewish knowledge, though most came from observant families. Although the records of their organizations were kept in German (and, as soon as possible, English), most seem to have used a Judeo-German jargon in conversation and for their private correspondence.[10]

In the 1830's the rate of emigration from Germany to the United States rose greatly, largely because of renewed economic and legal restrictions. The restrictions that some areas of Germany put on Jewish marriages led many young people to migrate to America in order to establish some form of family life. Others came to avoid conscription, to find personal freedom, or to achieve a level of economic security that was impossible in Germany.[11]

By the 1840's most of the German Jewish immigrants were steeped in general German culture, had been educated in secular schools, and were intensely devoted to German language and culture. Sermons were preached in German; scholarly works were written in German; and German language newspapers were published.[12] German was commonly used as the language of instruction in the schools (as Spanish or Portuguese had been used by the Sephardic Jews in Colonial times), and German was the spoken language in many Jewish homes.

Political views also changed with the times. Glazer and Moynihan point out that in New York City "German Jews, coming to political maturity and consciousness in the period of the Civil War, were perhaps predominantly Republican. Their preference for the Republicans on the national level coincided with their local interests, since the Democratic party, in the hands of the Irish, had no room for them".[13]

In the Jewish community, as with most of the German immigrants of the 19th century, there was an intense loyalty to the German nation. On April 23, 1903, Secretary of State John Hay sent the following comment to President Theodore Roosevelt: "It is a singular ethnological and political paradox that the prime motive of every British subject in America is hostility to England, and the prime motive of every German-American is hostility to every country in the world, including America, which is not friendly to Germany."[14]

Few of these immigrants had been assimilated into and accepted by German society, and they held social and commercial acceptance as one of their primary goals in America. Few had been members of the Reform movement in Germany, but many came to view Reform as "Americanized Judaism" and were soon drawn into the Reform movement in the United States.[15]

The enlightened German Jews who came to America after 1840 (and also those who fell in with the enlightenment after arriving) generally did not think of themselves as "Jews," but as "Israelites" or "Hebrews." The name "Jew" had sinister and distateful connotations in Germany. It was linked with legends of ritual murder, well-poisoning and, of course, Christ killing. "Jews" were the unenlightened, bearded masses of Eastern Europe. An "Israelite" was a gentleman "of Mosaic persuasion" whose culture and good manners suited him for brilliant conversation in the salons, made him love German language and culture, and placed him on a higher plane of existence than a "Jew."

This dislike for the term "Jew" was new to America. Reverence for Biblical ideas and a romatic fascination with the continuity of Jewish existence had been part of American life since Colonial days; and as late as 1823, editor Solomon Jackson called his monthly publication The Jew.[16] By 1854, Isaac Mayer Wise represented the thinking of a large segment of the German-born Jewish population by calling his newspaper The Israelite (later, The American Israelite); and in 1880 Rev. Sabato Morais, Italian-born rabbi of the Sephardic-Orthodox Congregation Mikveh Israel of Philadelphia, published a book entitled Eminent Israelites of the Nineteenth Century.

On March 9, 1883, Wise editorialized:

19

If you speak of Jews, you must not forget that there are
two kinds then, to be classified as Israelites and Jews. The
former are, as a class of people, known as believers in the
Old Testament, men and women who support congregations, public institutions of charity or instruction, visit
houses of worship and assist in cultivating and promulgating
the religious idea and advancing the cause of humanity. The
other class called Jews are persons who do nothing for the
benefit of man or the cause of Israel . . . This class of Jews
does not belong to us who are Israelites . . . They do not
recognize us and do not care for us, exactly as we do not
care for them . . . [17]

The Jews from Germany assimilated rapidly into American culture. Many were Americanized in half-a-generation; virtually all
were Americans, with only sympathies for Germany, by the first
native-born generation. The German-language Jewish press, which
had been strong in the 1850's to 1870's, numbered eleven in 1899,
one in 1914, and none by 1925.[18]

Government Actions

The American Jewish community of 1840 numbered only some
15,000.[19] By the time of World War I it numbered approximately
3,389,000, or 3.22% of the population.[20] Despite their relatively
small numbers, American Jews as individuals and as a community
felt secure in their rights and in their status as Americans. Only a
few had reservations about protesting injustices committed against
Jews either in the United States or abroad. Many felt it was not
only their right but their duty to petition the American government to amend its actions or intervene with a foreign government
when persecution or discrimination occurred.

In 1840, Mehemet Ali, the governor of Egypt, rebelled against
the Sultan of Turkey and took control of Syria and Palestine.

On February 5 of that year, Father Tomaso, head of the
Franciscan monastery in Damascus disappeared. The monks, led
by Father Tusti, who was already well known as an avid Jew-hater,
accused the Damascus Jewish community of having committed
ritual murder.[21] The French consul, who believed that this case
could be used to promote French interests, took personal charge
of the prosecution, and the rebel governor of Syria, Sherif Pasha,
incited Moslem mobs to anti-Jewish and anti-Turkish riots
throughout the Middle East. Protests were received from the
British and Austrian governments, nominally for humanitarian
reasons but really as a means of countering French ambitions; and
within France itself this became a hotly debated political issue.
Mehemet Ali soon realized that he had been drawn into the center
of a power struggle among the great European nations, and he

ordered a pardon and acquittal of all who had been convicted, in order to extricate himself from a precarious situation.

Reactions by the American Jewish community were widespread but fragmented. Meetings were held in all of the major Jewish communities and most of the smaller ones, both to protest the events in Damascus and to encourage the American government to take action. The reaction of the American government was strong and immediate. President Martin Van Buren had ordered a letter sent by Secretary of State John Forsyth even before the protest meetings began, and encouraged by the outspoken protests by both Jews and non-Jews, he kept up a stream of diplomatic correspondence until the case was finally resolved.[22]

Another incident in which the American Jewish community took a vital interest occurred in the Papal States. Edgar Mortara had been secretly baptized at the request of a servant girl who worked for the Mortara family when he was an infant. In June, 1858, he was forceably taken from his family and placed in the House of Catechumens (new converts) in Rome. The case had a strong impact throughout Europe and in the United States. The American Jewish community "responded with that exaggerated sensitivity to injustice which always characterizes the newly freed."

The American press carried many articles and editorials on the case, and the Anglo-Jewish press was unanimous both in their condemnation of the event and in their outspoken request for American governmental action. The first action, as it had been in the Damascus Affair, was the organization of protest meetings, from which petitions were sent to President James Buchanan and Secretary of State Lewis Cass, asking American intervention with the Pope. Initially the administration responded negatively to this request, but consistent pressure persuaded President Buchanan to issue a letter expressing his concern for Jewish sensibilities and his personal revulsion over the facts of the Mortara case. However, there was no change in United States government policy and no action taken to this case.[23]

In 1850 a proposed treaty between the United States and Switzerland included the provision that, because of the provisions of Swiss Canton law, only Christians were to have the rights specified. The Senate refused to ratify the treaty as presented.

Soon afterwards, however, a revised treaty was submitted which guaranteed equal treatment, but specified that federal, state or canton law was to prevail in all cases. This was the same kind of provision that had been included in the 1832 treaty with Russia. Since many of the Swiss cantons had restrictive laws against Jews, this provision only restated the earlier discrimination. The treaty in its revised form was approved by the Senate and declared in force by President Franklin Pierce in November, 1855.

Within a year the first case of restrictive canton law being applied to an American Jew was reported through the American ambassador, Theodore Fay. Protest meetings were held in many cities, and a conference held in Baltimore appointed a committee, led by Isaac Mayer Wise, which met with President James Buchanan in 1857. Finally, after long and fruitless negotiations between the two countries, the adoption of a Swiss federal constitution in 1874 finally overcame the restrictions and granted American Jews equal treatment as American citizens.[24]

Roumania had long been noted for the fierceness of its anti-Jewish restrictions. In 1870 President Grant appointed Benjamin Franklin Peixotto, the distinguished leader of B'nai B'rith, as American counsul-general in Roumania. Despite his efforts to relieve the plight of the Roumanian Jews during his six year tenure, little progress was made.

In 1878 Roumania gained her independence from Turkey as part of the Treaty of Berlin. One provision of her constitution provided that all inhabitants were entitled to citizenship. Between 1878 and 1900, however, only 85 Jews were made citizens.

In 1900-1906 an economic crisis hit Roumania, accompanied by the predictable increase of overt anti-Semitism, and some 70,000 Roumanian Jews emigrated to America. These Jews, most of whom lived as paupers in normal times, had been reduced to destitution; and their arrival caused great concern in America. In 1902 Secretary of State John Hay addressed a note to the countries which had participated in the Congress of Berlin, denouncing the Roumanian treatment of Jews both on humanitarian grounds and because it led to large-scale immigration of people whose entry was neither "acceptable or beneficial." Although many at first hailed this note as a symbol of America's humanitarian concerns, it brought about no improvement in the life of Roumanian Jews; and on closer reading, careful observers noted that it also served notice that America's traditional policy of unlimited immigration was being seriously questioned in the highest government circles.[25]

In 1832 the United States and Russia had concluded a Treaty of Commerce and Navigation, which included the provision that nationals of each country could trade in the other land on condition that they followed the regulations in force there. The implications of this provision were not realized until the 1860's, when special restrictions were placed on American Jews residing and doing business in Russia. By 1880 the severe restrictions placed on Russian Jews were applied to American Jews residing there. Extended diplomatic conversations did nothing to relieve the situation, and by 1893 it was discovered that the Russian consultates in the United States were refusing to grant visas to American Jews.

In May, 1907, in direct contradiction to the longstanding American policies that all citizens should be afforded equal protection while traveling abroad and that every person has the right of a voluntary expatriation, Secretary of State Elihu Root issued a "Notice to American Citizens Formerly Subjects of Russia Who Contemplate Returning to That Country." In this notice he warned that a naturalized American citizen who returned to Russia would be subject to treatment as if he were still a Russian citizen, and that passports would not be issued to Jews or to former Russian citizens without assurance that the Russian government would agree to their admission. This policy, which doubly restricted Russian Jewish immigrants, created great resentment in the American Jewish community, which by this time had developed a group-consciousness and a certain degree of organization.

Intervention by the American Jewish Committee brought about a modification in Root's "Notice," but President Theodore Roosevelt would not jeopardize American investments in Russia by pressing for revision or termination of the treaty. Finding that its usual method of dignified intervention was ineffective, the American Jewish Committee mounted a campaign in 1911 to arouse public indignation. Protests from political leaders and resolutions from organizations and state legislatures were sent to Washington. Resolutions calling for the abrogation of the treaty were reintroduced in both houses of Congress. Despite personal efforts by President William Howard Taft to convince leaders of the American Jewish community to call off their campaign, pressure continued throughout 1911. In December of that year, the House of Representatives, by a 300 to 1 vote, approved a resolution to abrogate the treaty; and before the Senate could consider a similar resolution reported unanimously by its Foreign Relations Committee, President Taft announced that in accordance with the provisions of the treaty, the United States would withdraw from the agreement on January 1, 1913.[26]

Organizations

By 1840, the American Jewish community considered itself an integral part of the American nation, fully entitled to request public recognition of its interests. It did not yet have, however, a well developed national group-consciousness, any organization that represented more than a small part of a single local community, or leaders of national stature who could rally the national community into action.

For the first time charity and social life left the confines of the synagogue. There were a few small organizations already in existence, and during the years of the German immigration many local organizations - - synagogues, social clubs, literary societies and philanthropies - - and several national organizations were established.

In New York City, for example, 35 permanently organized charities existed by 1860. Most served a specific purpose - - food, fuel, clothing, aid to widows, etc. - - and because they were extra-synagogal, each drew support from a cross-section of the Jewish community.[27] Funds for these charities came largely from socials, with the Purim Ball a special favorite. Unity came slowly, first in operations and later in fund raising. The United Hebrew Charities of New York City, founded in 1874, helped to coordinate the activities, but not the fund raising or policies, of its member organizations. The first move toward real unity came with the Federation movement, which started in Boston in 1895, spread to Cincinnati, Chicago, Philadelphia, Detroit, Cleveland, Buffalo, Indianapolis, Toledo, Louisville, Dayton, and San Francisco within fifteen years, and has since been adopted by most American Jewish communities.[28]

There were many social and card clubs formed during this period. Frequently, several clubs were founded by rival cliques, each vying for social supremacy. These clubs were often called Concordia or Harmonia, though there was little concord or harmony among the members of any of them.

The younger men established literary clubs (which later grew into the Young Men's Hebrew Association) in many cities. These clubs carried on a full program of book reviews, debates, lectures, poetry reading, elaborate "socials" and German songfests. Initially there was little Jewish content in their program; nor were there formal Americanization classes of the type provided for Russian immigrants a generation later, though Americanization was an important, if unstated, purpose of the societies.

On the national level, organization began in several areas. By the time of the Civil War, five Jewish fraternal orders had been established, of which only the B'nai B'rith has survived.[29] Founded in 1843 as a mutual aid society, by 1890 B'nai B'rith had expanded its activities to include a variety of philanthropic projects and activities for the protection of Jewish rights in both the United States and Europe. In 1913, to counter the rising tide of anti-Jewish feelings, the Anti-Defamation League of B'nai B'rith was founded to fill the need for systematic defense activity.[30]

The need for a representative body to speak and act on behalf of the entire American Jewish community had been clearly pointed up by the uncoordinated reactions to the Damascus Affair. Isaac Leeser led an unsuccessful attempt to organize such a body in 1841; in 1849, in cooperation with Isaac Mayer Wise, he tried again; and a national conference of rabbis convened in 1855 quickly broke up because of the antagonism between Reform and Orthodox elements.

A year after the Mortara Case the first moderately successful organization came into existence. The Board of Delegates of American Israelites was called together in November, 1859, by Rabbi Samuel M. Isaacs of New York. The Board of Delegates was hampered by the non-participation of the leading Reform and Sephardic congregations, which did not favor a separate, non-synagogal organization as spokesman for the American Jewish community. The Board of Delegates functioned until 1878, when it was absorbed into the Union of American Hebrew Congregations as the Board of Delegates on Civil and Religious Rights. The Jewish Alliance of America, founded in 1891 for the same purposes, disbanded after only one year.

Inspired in part by the outbreak of pogroms in Russia, the American Jewish Committee held its first meeting in New York City in November, 1906. The Committee, which represented the wealthy, conservative, Americanized "German" group, set as its goals the protection of the civil and religious rights of Jews and the giving of relief to Jews who suffered persecution. Although it initially was strongly anti-Zionist, by the end of World War I it actively cooperated with the Jewish Agency, and by 1947 advocated a Jewish national home in Palestine as a refuge for the persecuted Jews of Europe. In 1914, the American Jewish Relief Committee, sponsored by the American Jewish Committee, was one of the three agencies which merged into the American Jewish Joint Distribution Committee (JDC)[31] for relief work in Europe. The Committee was one of the Jewish groups which sent a delegation to Versailles to work for the inclusion of provisions in the treaty which would protect the rights of minority nationalities (a term which was also applied to the Jews). Although the Committee's efforts were relatively ineffective at Versailles (as were the efforts of all Jewish delegations), the fact that the United States government thought them important enough to be included as a part of the American delegation made this a significant event in American Jewish history.

Beginning at the time of World War I, interest arose, especially among the disenfranchised "Russians," in the formation of a democratically elected American Jewish Congress, which would replace the oligarchic "German" American Jewish Committee. The first meeting of the Congress, held in Philadelphia in December,

1918, included 400 delegates. This meeting adopted a three-point program: to send a delegation to the Versailles Conference; to cooperate with the World Zionist Organization in working for the establishment of a Jewish national home in Palestine; and to work for the legal recognition of the civil rights and liberties of Jews in all countries.

Economic Life

"From 1848 to 1880, the German Jew reigned supreme in American Jewish life, owing to his superiority in numbers, his intellectual powers, his wealth, and his public spirit."[32] The expansion of industry, the growth of cities and the development of the West provided almost unlimited opportunities for those with daring and ingenuity.

In Germany, Jews had occupied a variety of occupations in the middle and lower levels of the economic scale. In addition to the usual occupations of money-lending, peddling, and marketing used clothing and furniture, Jews were often employed as commercial agents by land owners and the owners of large businesses.[33] This varied background equipped the new immigrants well for life in an expanding America, and the skills a man brought with him often determined where he settled.[34]

Because most of the immigrants came with little capital, and also because most were accustomed to being businessmen rather than factory or agricultural workers, many began their careers as peddlers. While many remained in the major East Coast cities, many followed the westward movement of the American population. Some settled in the growing river towns of Pittsburgh, Cincinnati, Louisville, Cairo, Memphis, St. Louis and New Orleans. Many went to the new manufacturing and commercial centers: Boston, Cleveland, Newark, Detroit, Milwaukee, and Chicago. Others ventured farther west into Utah, Colorado, Oklahoma, Texas, and California.

As a peddler with a pack on his back or a covered wagon filled with trinkets and household products, the Jewish peddler followed closely behind the agricultural pioneer. Almost anything that was salable was his stock in trade. Often he was the only contact between the pioneer settler and civilization, bringing news along with products. In many cases some settlers saw a Jew for the first time in the peddler who came to their home. As the settlements grew more dense in the West, the Jewish peddler saw it to his advantage to move his center of business operations into their midst. "The fortunes of the Jew and the steady progress of his neighbors were thus firmly bound together. The settlement grew into a village and the peddler's depot became a dry-goods store;

the town grew into a city and a department store occupied the very center of its Main Street."[35]

Starting as a basket-peddler, the ambitious immigrant usually progressed to the status of pack-peddler, who often carried 150 pounds of merchandise on his back. If his business prospered, he could purchase a horse and wagon to carry his wares or settle down as the owner of a small store, usually in clothing and notions.[36] "The merchandise of the peddler was sold for a profit, small reserves were accumulated, greater economic opportunities were sought out, a store was rented, real estate was purchased, and new ventures were explored. Partnerships were formed, small businesses expanded, and often the profits were invested in the development of railraods, coal, quarries, lumbering, oil, or factories."[37]

Many of the prominent Jewish families of America owe their beginnings to an ancestor who was a peddler, rag-picker, junk dealer, fruit huckster, second-hand clothing dealer, pawnbroker, tailor, shoemaker, baker, cabinet maker, watchmaker, or cigar maker. These were the men who rose from very modest beginnings to be owners of large stores, and whose sons and grandsons became leaders of the giant department store chains, manufacturing firms or banking houses. This group was eager to achieve success, and had the energy, daring and ingenuity to be successful. In this group of German Jewish immigrants belong many of the distinguished American Jewish families: the Seligmans; Solomon Loeb and Jacob H. Schiff of Kuhn, Loeb and Company; Benjamin Altman of the Altman department stores; the Gimbel Brothers of New York; the Lazarus family of Columbus, Ohio; the Warburg family; the Guggenheims; Otto H. Kahn; and Adolph S. Ochs of *The New York Times.* "The father of the famous Straus brothers - - Oscar, Nathan, and Isidor - - came from Germany in 1852, peddled with horse and wagon through the South, and opened a store in Georgia. From such humble beginnings came Macy's in New York, and Abraham and Straus, in Brooklyn. The sons Isidor and Oscar had notable careers as public servants and philanthropists. Among the intellectual leaders of this group of German Jews coming either from Germany or Austria may be mentioned the Goldmarks, the Dembitz, Brandeis, and Adler families, Isaac M. Wise, the Flexners, the Untermeyers, the Frankfurters, and many others."[38]

Having achieved success and economic stability, they adhered to the pattern of other successful immigrant groups. After the German Jewish parents laid the financial foundations, their children attended college, had the time to devote to the various professions and to participate in civic affairs. They pioneered in and supported the arts, engaged in publishing, scholarship and the entertainment industry. The significant careers of Jews in public service manifests the German Jews' capacity to profit from the social and educational opportunities the United States had to offer them.[39]

The War Between the States

Between 1800 and 1860 the last vestiges of legal discrimination against Jews were removed in all states except New Hampshire, where the Christian oath for legislators remained in force until 1876.[40] The Jewish population had grown to about 150,000 (of a total white population of 27,000,000) and had gained political acceptance in most states. David Emanuel, a hero of the siege of Savannah during the Revolutionary War, was elected governor of Georgia in 1801. Six Jews served in the Congress of the United States: Senators David Levy Yulee, Florida, 1845-51 and 1855-61; and Judah Philip Benjamin, Louisiana, 1853-61; and Representatives Lewis Charles Levin, Pennsylvania, 1845-51; Emanuel B. Hart, New York, 1851-53; Philip Philips, Alabama, 1853-55; and Henry Myer Philips, Pennsylvania, 1857-59.[41]

When the War began, the Jewish community split North and South, as did the rest of the country;[42] and all shades of opinion were represented among the leadership of the Jewish community. Isidor Bush, publisher of *Israel's Herold;* Moritz Pinner, publisher of the *Kansas Post;* and Ernestine Rose, the suffragette leader, were leading abolitionists. Rabbi David Einhorn was so outspoken against slavery that he had to flee for his life from pro-slavery vigilantes in Baltimore, and spent the rest of his career in Philadelphia. Michael Heilprin, a new immigrant who had been active in the 1848 Revolution in Hungary, became famous because of his published refutations of pro-slavery arguments. Up to 1861, Rabbi Max Lilienthal of Cincinnati was in favor of allowing each state to decide the slavery question for itself; but once the War began, he became an outspoken Unionist and a supporter of Lincoln. Taking the pro-slavery view were such men as Rabbis J. M. Michelbacher and George Jacobs of Richmond, Mordecai M. Noah and Dr. Morris J. Raphall of New York, whose pro-slavery sermon was widely reprinted. Yulee and Bejamin left the Senate to work for the Confederacy, and Army Major Alfred Mordecai of North Carolina, Commander of the Washington Arsenal and noted for his research in artillery and ballistics, resigned his commission rather than fight against the South. Many of the journalist-rabbis were equivocal. Isaac M. Wise of Cincinnati condemned both slavery and the abolitionists who, he contended, were power-hungry politicians responsible for starting the War and would attack the Jews next. Others shared his views and fears. Samuel M. Isaacs of New York condemned Einhorn's political activism, but like Isaac Leeser of Philadelphia would not comment on the slavery question.

When the War began, Jewish organizations and individuals throughout the Union contributed their full support. Some 15,000 served in the Union Army. Jews at home showed their support by collecting money and clothing, packing supplies and bandages, and holding fund-raising socials and Sanitary Fairs (named for the United States Sanitary Commission, re-named in 1882 The Red Cross). Several wards of Jews' Hospital (later changed to Mt. Sinai Hospital) in New York were turned into a military hospital, and the families of Jewish soldiers were supported by Jewish communal charities. Financiers August Belmont and Joseph Seligman raised some $200,000,000 for the Union through loans and the sale of Federal securities in Europe.

As in all times of political and economic stress, when the demand for conformity becomes a dimension of nationalism, anti-Jewish feelings grew during the war. Senator Henry Wilson (later vice-president under Grant), Senator Andrew Johnson (later president), and "Parson" William G. Brownlow (a popular evangelist and "Know Nothing" supporter) gave anti-Jewish speeches. Newspapers were careful to point out the religion of any Jew who was arrested or active in the Confederacy, and they often asserted that Jewish bankers, led by Belmont, were secretly financing the Confederacy. Military leaders such as Colonel Lafayette C. Baker, chief of the Detective Service of the War Department, General Benjamin F. Butler, known as "Beast Butler" because of his severe rule as military governor of New Orleans, and General Ulysses S. Grant, whose infamous Order No. 11 expelled all Jews from the Department of the Tennessee, were openly anti-Jewish.

Not everyone shared these attitudes. President Lincoln had many Jewish friends and was sympathetic to the plight of the Jews. Grant's Order No. 11 was rescinded by presidential order as soon as word reached Washington. Through Lincoln's influence, the "Christian clergy" provision of the military chaplaincy law was reinterpreted to permit the immediate appointment of rabbis as hospital chaplains, and later as field chaplains.

The Jews of the South proved to be devoted sons of the Confederacy. Between 10,000 and 12,000 were in military service. Many more engaged in supplying the food, money and goods needed to conduct the war - - both by legal trading and, when necessary, by smuggling through Union blockades. Judah P. Benjamin, having quit the Senate, became a leader in the Confederate government, rising to Secretary of State by the end of the War; and A.C. Myers served as Quartermaster-General to the Army.

As in the North, anti-Jewish feelings built up; and as the antici- pated victory turned into defeat, Jews were an available scapegoat on whom all failures could be blamed. Confederate Congressman Henry S. Foote, (who deserted the Confederacy and escaped to the Union in 1865) was most outspoken, and he was joined by others as the War progressed. Nativism and religious resentment were probably stronger in the fundamentalist Christian South than it was in the North, and this basic distrust of Jews made stories of profiteering, subversion, and treason more believable. Judah P. Benjamin, a favorite target of the North, fell into particular dis- favor also in the South and was blamed for all the problems of the Confederacy.

The War between the States brought no great changes in the American Jewish community that were not reflections of America-at-large. However, it was an important era. It demon- strated, on the one hand, the degree to which the Jewish com- munity was Americanized and committed to a variety of "American" points of view. On the other hand, it brought out and focused the anti-foreign and anti-Jewish sentiments (which were to become stronger and more overt from the end of the Civil War until the outbreak of World War II) latent in America, and it multiplied and intensified the personal and institutional rivalries that already existed among the leadership of the Jewish com- munity.

Social Integration and Anti-Semitism

During the first half of the 19th century, the attitude of Christian Americans toward Jews was generally quite friendly. Americans in general were distraught at the treatment of Jews in the various European countries, and on many public occasions expressed a willingness to have the oppressed Jews of Europe come to live in the United States.[43] In part this feeling was at- tributable to "American Ideals" and in part to the fact that the American Jewish community was so small as to be almost invisi- ble. Many Americans outside the major east coast cities had never even seen a Jew.

There were scattered anti-Jewish incidents during these years. Commodore Uriah P. Levy, a fourth generation American, was known as "the damned Jew" to his class-conscious fellow naval officers during his stormy career.[44] By the 1850's Shylock-type Jewish characters were not uncommon on the stage and in car- toons, and the use of "to Jew" as a verb meaning "to cheat by unfair business practices" was a common occurrence in the American slang vocabulary. Throughout this period, however, there were few acts of overt, organized anti-Semitism.

During the War between the States, anti-Jewish feelings crystallized in the reactions of Union Generals Grant and Sherman; and using Judah P. Benjamin[45] as a prototype of Jewish infidelity, the Northern press on occasion attacked the Jewish community as a whole. The Southern press, on the other hand, found occasion to condemn Jews for the Confederate Army's lack of supplies and equipment.

Following the war, overt anti-Semitism sharply increased. Among the hatreds of the Ku Klux Klan, the Jew was not excluded. In the North, where a number of Jews were a part of the "New-Rich" society, anti-Jewish feelings were expressed primarily in the form of social exclusiveness. The most publicized incident, though not the first such case, came in 1877. Joseph Seligman, one of America's leading financiers, was denied accommodations at the fashionable Grand Union Hotel in Saratoga Springs, New York. Because of Seligman's prominence, the case drew national attention. The *New York Times* headlined their first article, "A Sensation at Saratoga."[46] Other "watering-holes" soon followed the Grand Union's lead, and such signs as "No Jews or Dogs Admitted" sprung up in many resort areas. Many clubs, colleges and fashionable private schools either excluded Jews or set up quotas limiting the number of Jews they would admit. Even inexpensive boarding houses in such favorite resorts as the Catskills "restricted" their clientele.[47] Jews in many locales established their own resorts and social clubs, which were usually more plush than those from which they were excluded.

Education

The Sunday School was the educational institution which Reform Jews adopted and developed to train their children. It met on Sunday morning for about one and a half to two and a half hours. Its course of study consisted of Bible, history, Jewish religion and customs, Jewish current events, singing, and Hebrew. Due to the limitation of time as well as to the philosophy of Reform Judaism, Hebrew did not occupy a central place in the curriculum.[48] Age of admission to the Sunday school was eight years old, and there were five grades which eventually led to confirmation for both boys and girls around the age of thirteen. This followed the practice started in the Reform congregations of Germany and was a definite break with Orthodox tradition, in which each boy (but never a girl) had an individual *bar mitzvah* at his thirteenth birthday.[49]

As long as public schools were taking care of secular knowledge, Jewish congregations felt that they only needed to provide facilities for religious education. Therefore, congregations did not feel obligated to maintain private schools and pay salaries to teach the children what they could learn in the public schools.[50]

The Orthodox Congregation Mikveh Israel of Philadelphia started the first Sunday School in the United States in 1832. In 1838, Congregation Beth Elohim in Charleston, South Carolina, organized the first Sunday school founded by a Reform Congregation in America. It was among the Reform Jews that the Sunday School movement went on. The Sunday School achieved some success during the latter half of the nineteenth century, but among the Orthodox Jews from Eastern Europe who immigrated in the period beginning with the 1880's and ending around 1920, the Sunday School movement did not gain much popularity.

Ever since 1838 Sunday Schools, plus an occasional afternoon Hebrew school, were to remain the typical method of Jewish education in the United States till the twentieth century. After 1910, afternoon schools, under the influence of the new bureaus of Jewish education, were founded in order to produce a synthesis of Jewish history, American pedagogy and Zionistic ethnicism. [51] The acceptance of Zionism was influenced by American Jewish reaction to the Russia pogroms and to the anti-Semitic excesses of the later nineteenth and early twentieth century in Western as well as Eastern Europe. Many Reform Jewish leaders were especially effected by these acts of anti-Semitism.[52]

In an attempt to give direction to the Sunday Schools which were increasing all over the United States, the Hebrew Sabbath School Union of America was organized in Cincinnati in 1886. The constitution of the organization, adopted at its first meeting, stated that its object was "to provide a uniform system for all Hebrew Sabbath Schools in the United States by promulgating a uniform course of instruction and by training competent teachers." Rabbi David Philipson of Cincinnati was elected its president. During its short existence, this organization published textbooks and leaflets, set up curriculums for religious schools and teacher training programs, and emphasized the importance of religious education for Jewish life. The Sabbath School Union functioned until 1903, when it merged with the Union of American Hebrew Congregations. Its work was then taken over by the Commission on Jewish Education, a joint commission of the Union of American Hebrew Congregations and the Central Conference of American Rabbis.[53]

Another producer of educational materials was the Jewish Chautauqua Society, founded by Henry Berkowitz in 1893, which published teaching materials and established a correspondence school for teachers. The Gratz College in Philadelphia, founded in 1895, was the first institution under Jewish auspices to be devoted entirely to the training of teachers. In 1909, teacher training institutes were added to Hebrew Union College and the Jewish Theological Seminary.

The Reform Movement

Reform Judaism was the gift of the German immigrant to the American Jewish community. Although the movement was born in Germany, it found its home in America. Throughout the 19th century, Reform was the dominant American Jewish cultural force. Because its universalist, humanitarian ideals matched so well the ideals of 19th century America, it represented more the Americanization than the modernization of the Jewish tradition.

Until the time of the French Revolution and the rise of Napoleon, the European Jewish community (with the exception of Holland and certain eras in other countries) lived in forced isolation from the non-Jewish world.[54] As the army of Napoleonic France swept across the continent, a period of emancipation arrived for the Jews of Europe. The Jews, now treated as citizens, began to move toward cultural assimilation along the lines advocated earlier by Moses Mendelssohn: by becoming familiar with the culture and customs of their country, in order to "prove" to their non-Jewish fellow countrymen that they could be "worthy citizens" whose conduct and nationalism were above reproach.[55]

The Reform Movement began with the efforts of German laymen to adapt Judaism to the "enlightened" world outside the ghetto. Despite strong opposition from the orthodox element, often assisted by state authorities after the Congress of Vienna restored conservative governments to power, Reform continued and made a certain amount of progress.

One of the chief obstacles that Reform had to overcome was the long-standing custom that any change in Jewish religious belief or practice could be justified only by reinterpretation of the existing tradition. Reform believed that changes made for the sake of modernization were legitimate even without recourse to reinterpretation. Because the Reformers wanted to stay within this historic Jewish continuum and not become merely sectarians, they developed a new, critical approach to the study of the Jewish past, its traditions, modes of belief and basic principles. Under the leadership of such men as Abraham Geiger and Leopold Zunz, the *Wissenschaft des Judenthums* (Science of Judaism) utilized the finest techniques of German scholarship to analyze and reinterpret the Jewish past.

The schools opened by the Reform Movement throughout Germany served as both educational centers and testing grounds for innovations in the religious services. The synygogues founded - -

which were called "temples" to signify that they no longer looked forward to the restoration of the Jerusalem Temple and its priestly worship - - incorporated many changes in religious practice. Among the most significant changes were the introduction of a weekly sermon and the reading of some parts of the service in the vernacular; the use of instrumental music; seating in family pews; allowing men to pray without head covering and prayer shawl; observance of strict decorum; and the abbreviation of the service by eliminating the repetition of certain prayers and the saying of all prayers for the return to Zion, the restoration of the sacrificial cult, the resurrection of the dead, and the coming of a personal messiah.

To bring about some degree of uniformity in beliefs and practices, conferences were held in which both rabbis and laymen discussed and reached a common position on many of the crucial religious problems facing the newly emancipated Jews.[56]

Between 1820 and 1850 the Reform movement made little progress except academically and educationally. Scholars worked to legitimize the changes that had already been made; and in the schools, where secular as well as religious subjects were taught, the most modern educational techniques were utilized.

By 1848, when reactionary governments moved strongly against all liberal movements, Reform had lost its momentum in Germany. The Reform Movement had begun during a time of enforced liberalism and had offered, for a while, an approach to Judaism that was based on the most modern ideals and attuned to current realities. It had told the Jews coming out of the ghetto that if they modernized themselves, they could become full and equal citizens of Germany. Beginning with the conservatism that followed the Congress of Vienna and reaching a climax in the repressions that followed the unsuccessful revolution of 1848, the promise of Reform no longer matched the actual conditions of German life. As reaction set in and anti-Semitism again grew strong and open, Jews were among those who suffered most. Even those who had "modernized" were again the scapegoats on whom fell the blame for all the ills of society.

By this time, however, large numbers of Germany Jews had already emigrated to America; and in the first years of the reaction more joined them. Among these migrants were many Reformers, including most of the rabbis who led the development of the Reform movement in the United States.

In America the liberal premises and hopeful promises of Reform coincided with the realities of society; and it was in America alone that Reform grew into a powerful national movement.

In America, as in Europe, laymen initiated the Reform movement. In 1824, some twenty years before the great immigration of

34

German Jews made possible the development of a viable Reform movement, forty-seven members of the Beth Elohim Congregation of Charleston, South Carolina, petitioned their governing board to allow certain segments of the service to be conducted in the English language and to have the entire service shortened. When the petition was rejected, twelve members seceded from the Beth Elohim Congregation and organized the "Reformed Society of Israelites."

The Charleston Reformers stated that it was their purpose to free themselves from the ritual laws of rabbinical Judaism and center their movement on the moral legislation in the Bible. The Reformed Society stressed the ideals which typified the Reform Movement: monotheism, immortality of the soul, good will toward all men as being the children of God, the use of English as well as Hebrew, the omission of all prayers for the coming of the Messiah and for the resurrection of the dead, the use of instrumental music, mixed seating and the uncovering of heads when worshiping. In 1830, the Reformed Society published the first congregational Reform prayer-book in America. However, the Reformed Society lasted only a few years.

Beth Elohim Congregation invited Gustav Posnanski to be its rabbi in 1836. Posnanski, a native of Hamburg, was influenced by the reforms of the Hamburg Temple and introduced many reforms into the worship service. After a fire destroyed the building of Beth Elohim Congregation a few years later, a pipe organ was installed in the new edifice. When the temple was dedicated in 1841, it became the first permanent Reform congregation in the United States. At the dedication ceremony Rabbi Posnanski said, "This synagogue is our Temple, this city our Jerusalem, this happy land our Palestine."[57]

Many of the most fervent proponents of Reform left Germany at this time and came to America. They were disappointed at the poor results that the Reform Movement had achieved in Europe, and they believed that in America, where Reform would be unhampered by the dead weight of communal tradition and the interference of a reactionary government, Reform Judaism could prosper.[58] The American Reform movement was strongly influenced by the "enlightened," assimilationist program of the Reform movement in Germany, and it carried on the idealist philosophy which dominated 19th century Germany thought. Among the Reform leaders who immigrated to the United States at this time were many of the rabbis who led in the development of the movement: David Einhorn, Max Lilienthal, Samuel Adler, Bernard Felsenthal, Samuel Hirsch, and Isaac Mayer Wise.[59]

It was Isaac Mayer Wise who was most prominent in the growth

and organization of Reform Judaism in the United States.[60] Wise
believed that Jewish fortunes and American fortunes were tied
together; he was an American nationalist in thought and spirit. [61]
He believed that essential Judaism and essential Americanism are
alike: rational, ethical, and humanitarian. He saw America as the
land of hope and promise for the Jew, not only because it offered
economic and political opportunity,[62] but also because it offered
the Jew a spiritual home, a place where he could revitalize his
religion without feat of restraint. Wise believed that the American
Judaism which he taught was not a mixture of two distinct parts,
the Jewish and the American; he believed, rather, that at their
highest and best, Americanism and Judaism are one.[63] He later
wrote: "This country approaches nearest the Mosaic state among
all the countries known in history."[64]

Wise further believed that both Orthodox Christianity, with its
strict other-worldly dogmatism, and Orthodox Judaism, with its
"Orientalism" and emphasis on rituals, were divisive and
obscurantist. He dreamed of replacing both with a pure, sane,
idealistic universal faith - - i.e., Reform Judaism.[65]

After being dismissed as rabbi of the congreation in Albany,
New York, because of the reforms he tried to introduce, Wise
formed a Reform congregation there in 1850. Soon afterward he
removed to Cincinnati, where he ministered to Congregations Bene
Israel and B'nai Jeshurun, which adopted Reform in 1854 and
1855. It was in Cincinnati that he found the support necessary to
begin organizing the Reform movement. Wise was very moderate
in his approach to Reform. *Minhag Amerika,* the prayer book he
compiled, modified the orthodox liturgy only to eliminate repeti-
tions and to conform to Reform views on such subjects as immortality, Zionism and messianism. His goal was to unite all
American Jews into one movement, and he saw both radical Reform and orthodoxy as obstacles to be overcome in attaining his
goal. His following came primarily from the mid-west and the
south, and he often commented bitterly on the "Easterners" - -
both Reform and Orthodox - - who would not accept his ideas
and his leadership. It was in spite of Wise, not because of him, that
the Reform rabbinical conferences adopted radical platforms and
the prayer book officially adopted by the Reform movement was
greatly different from the traditional liturgy.

As it had in Germany, the American Reform movement grew
differently in each congregation. Also as in Germany, leaders of
Reform soon assembled in conference to work out a common
position on important issues. The first American conference was
held in Philadelphia in 1869. The chairman of the conference was
Rabbi Samuel Hirsh, who was philosophically conservative but
liberal in religion. A dominant force in the conference was Rabbi

David Einhorn, the radical religious and social reformer whose *Olat Tamid* was the basis on which the *Union Prayer Book* of the Reform movement was built.

Unlike the European conferences, all thirteen participants were rabbis, and no laymen were invited. The declaration of principles which they adopted reiterated the universalistic ideals on which the German movement had been founded: that the messianic ideal of Israel[66] is the union of all men as children of God; that Israel was dispersed throughout the world to lead the nations to the true knowledge and worship of God; that Israel does not look to the restoration of the sacrificial cult or of Palestine as a Jewish home-land; that distinctions between priests, Aaronites and Jews-in-general are no longer valid; that the selection of Israel as the people chosen to be the bearer of God's will should be stressed; that immortality refers only to the existence of the soul after death; and that worship should be conducted in a language which the worshipers can understand.[67]

At Wise's instigation, representatives of Reform congregations met in Cincinnati in 1873 and established the Union of American Hebrew Congregations. Under the sponsorship of UAHC, the Hebrew Union College was founded in 1875 for the training of American rabbis. The graduates of this seminary, along with European-trained Reform rabbis serving American congregations formed the Central Conference of American Rabbis in 1889.[68] Wise served as president of all these groups until his death in 1900.

In 1885 a conference was held in Pittsburgh to reformulate the principles of the Reform movement. Wise served as chairman of the conference, but the dominant voice was Rabbi Kaufmann Kohler, a radical reformer who later succeeded Wise as president of Hebrew Union College and guided its development into a major center of Jewish scholarship. He wrote the platform that was adopted, and his supporters formed a majority of the delegates.

The "Pittsburgh Platform" recognized the fact that all religions attempt to grasp the God-idea, but it stressed that Judaism maintained this idea as the central religious truth for the human race; that the Bible is the chief instrument of moral instruction and modern scientific discoveries are not antagonistic to the doctrines of Judaism; that the Mosaic legislation is binding only in its moral laws, and all ceremonies that are contrary to the views and habits of modern civilization are rejected; that all Mosaic and rabbinical laws that regulate diet and dress are rejected as being obstructive to modern spiritual elevation; that Jews do not consider them-selves a nation but members of a religious community, and there-fore do not expect a return to Palestine; that Judaism is a progressive religion striving to be in accord with the postulates of reason, and it recognizes Christianity and Islam as being daughter-religions of Judaism; that in the doctrine of Judaism the soul is immortal, and the idea of Hell and Paradise as abodes for ever-lasting punishment and rewards is not rooted in Judaism; and that the Jew strives to participate in the tasks of modern times through solving the problems presented by the present organization of society.[69]

The "Pittsburgh Platform" was not an official pronouncement, since it was issued before the formation of the Central Conference of American Rabbis, but it came to be regarded as the authoritative Reform position for the next 50 years.

The Reform movement grew rapidly and during the 19th century seemed on its way to becoming the dominant movement in American Judaism. The immigration of large numbers of East European Jews, who settled primarily in the East and scorned Reform, changed the composition of the religious community and limited the influence of both Reform and the Mid-west.

The Traditionalists

Because so many of the German immigrants had belonged to the Orthodox movement in Germany, it is natural that many affiliated with traditional synagogues in America. Especially in the large cities of the East, traditional Judaism found great support. The first German-rite synagogue was Congregation Rodeph Shalom of Philadelphia, founded in 1802. By 1850,, twenty of the 77 Jewish congregations in New York followed the German ritual. This indicated both the increased number of German immigrants and the divisiveness which characterized the American Jewish community at this time. These congregations slowly introduced changes in traditional practices, as did their Sephardic counter-parts.

Not one of the Reformers, but the Orthodox Rabbi Isaac Leeser of Philadelphia was the first to preach sermons in English. In 1830, his second year as leader of Congregation Mikveh Israel, he found that the already-Americanized members of his congregation were most comfortable when he spoke in English. Many of the families had been in America since colonial times, and they knew neither the Spanish and Portugese of their forebearers nor his own native German. In New York, Rabbi Samuel M. Isaacs, the first rabbi of a German-ritual synagogue in America, introduced the English sermon at Bene Yeshurun synagogue ten years later.

Leeser was also a leader in many attempts both to reflect and to further the Americanization of the Jewish community. In 1832 the first Jewish Sunday School, patterned after the Protestant Bible Schools, was opened at Mikveh Israel under the direction of Rebecca Gratz. Leeser was active in the first attempt to found an

American Jewish Publication Society; was president of Maimonides College, the first attempt to establish an American rabbinical seminary (opened in October, 1867; closed in 1873 because of financial problems); published an Anglo-Jewish monthly, *The Occident;* and produced a Hebrew-English prayer book (1848) and an English translation of the Hebrew Scriptures (1853), which was the standard American Jewish version until 1917.[70]

A second, this time successful, attempt to found a traditional seminary in America came in January, 1887. Wise's Hebrew Union College, founded twelve years earlier, proved unacceptable to the traditionalist "Easterners" both because of its Reform approach (as exemplified by the ideas of the Pittsburgh Platform) and because it was located in "the West." The Jewish Theological Seminary of America[71] was founded in New York City. Sabato Morais, who had succeeded Lesser as rabbi of Mikveh Israel, was named president, a post he held until his death in 1897.[72] Under Morais, and later under the distinguished scholar Solomon Schechter,[73] this institution became the center of the new Conservative, or historical-critical, movement.[74] Following the pattern of the Reform movement, graduates of the Seminary associated in the Rabbinical Assembly of America (1901), and congregations affiliated with the Conservative movement joined together to form the United Synagogue of America (1913). The program of the movement, as outlined by Schechter in 1913, was aimed at promoting traditional Jewish observance and allowing room for moderate change. In opposition to the official policy of the Reform movement, it strongly supported the newly-formed Zionist movement.

Similar organizations were formed in the Orthodox movement after the waves of Russian immigrants had increased its strength. In 1902 the Agudas Harabonim (Union of Orthodox Rabbis) was formed to strengthen traditional religious observance and to supervise the religious regulations pertaining to marriage and divorce. One of the seminaries they supported was the Rabbi Isaac Elchanan Theological Seminary, which grew under the leadership of Bernard Revel and his successor, Samuel Belkin, into Yeshivah University and now includes the Albert Einstein Medical Center. In 1930 the Rabbinical Council of America, made up mostly of graduates of the Yeshivah, was founded by the younger, American-trained orthodox rabbis, and the Union of Orthodox Jewish Congregations allied with it.[75]

FOOTNOTES

For The German Period

1. For a biography see: *The Jewish Encyclopedia* (New York: Funk and Wagnalls, 1904), Vol. VIII, pp. 479-485.
2. M. J. Landa, *The Jew in Drama* (London: P. S. King and Son, Ltd., 1926), pp. 254-260. See also: Sylvan D. Schwartzman, *Reform Judaism in the Making* (New York: Union of American Hebrew Congregations, 1962), p. 21; Heinrich Graetz, *History of the Jews* (Philadelphia: The Jewish Publication Society of America, 1895), Vol. V. pp. 325-327.
3. Abraham Cronbach, *Reform Movements in Judaism* (New York: Bookman Associates, Inc., 1963), p. 109.
4. See: Selma Stern-Taeubler, "The Motivation of the German Jewish Emigration to America in the Post-Mendelssohnian Era," *Essays in American Jewish History* (Cincinnati: The American Jewish Archives, 1958), pp. 247-252.
5. Article XVI of the Treaty of Vienna as originally drafted specified that Jews were to be given "rights as heretofore accorded them *in* the several states" - - *i.e.,* including those decreed by Napoleon. The final form of the treaty contained the provision that Jews were to be given only those rights granted "*by* the several states" - - *i.e.,* only those rights granted by the "legitimate" rulers of each state, and not including those decreed by Napoleon during the years of his rule. This facilitated the restoration of restrictions on Jews in many areas.
6. For details see: Koppel S. Pinson, *Modern Germany,* 2nd edition (New York: The Macmillan Company, 1966), pp. 62-67.
7. *American Jewish Year Book 5660* (1899-1900), (Philadelphia. The Jewish Publication Society of America, 1899), p. 283.
8. Nathaniel Weyl, *The Jew in American Politics* (New Rochelle, New York: Arlington House, 1968), p. 37.
9. Joseph L. Blau and Salo W. Baron, ed. *The Jews of the United States, 1790-1840: A Documentary History* (New York: Columbia University Press, and Philadelphia: Jewish Publication Society of America, 1963). Vol. I, p. 86.
10. Bernard D. Weinryb, "The German Jewish Immigrants to America (A Critical Evaluation)," *Jews from Germany in the United States,* Eric E. Hirshler, ed. (New York: Farrar, Straus and Cudahy, 1955), pp. 103-105, 113-126).
11. Blau and Baron, Vol. III, pp. 803-805.
12. For a list of German language periodicals see: Adolph Kober, "Aspects of the Influence of Jews from Germany on American Jewish Spiritual Live of the Nineteenth Century," *Jews from Germany in the United States,* Eric E. Hirshler, ed., (New York: Farrar, Straus and Cudahy, 1955), p. 133.
13. Nathan Glazer and Daniel Patrick Moynihan, *Beyond the Melting Pot* (Cambridge, Massachusetts: The M.I.T. Press, 1964), pp. 168-169.
14. Quoted in Hans Kohn, *American Nationalism* (New York: Collier Books, 1957), p. 169.
15. See: Oscar Handlin, *The Uprooted* (New York: Grosset and Dunlap Publishers, 1951), p. 141.
16. See: Sol Liptzin, *Generation of Decision* (New York: Bloch Publishing Co., 1958), pp. 74-82.
17. Quoted in Dena Wilansky, *Sinai to Cincinnati* (New York: Renaissance Book Co., 1937), p. 175.
18. *American Jewish Year Book 5660 (1899-1900),* 271-282; *5675 (1914-1915),* pp. 328-334; *5676 (1915-1916),* pp. 340-341; *5686 (1925-1926),* pp. 355-362.
19. *American Jewish Year Book 5660 (1899-1900),* p. 283.
20. *American Jewish Year Book 5680 (1919-1920),* p. 606.
21. The "ritual murder" or "blood libel" charge against Jews was a frequent occurence in the medieval period and recurred off and on after that. The accusation made was that a Jew had killed a Christian in order to use his blood for some ritual purpose. Since these accusations arose often around Easter, when anti-Jewish feelings and actions were aroused to their highest peak by the crucifixion stories recounted in the churches, the supposed ritual use was related to the Jewish holiday of Pesach (Passover), which also occurs in the Spring. Despite frequent refutations - - including most obviously the fact that Jewish religious law

prohibits the eating of blood and even prescribes the method for totally removing the blood from ritually slaughtered meat so that it will be *kosher* (proper for use) - - the charge has had amazing lasting-power and a seemingly limitless appeal to those who are prepared to hate Jews.

22. See: Cyrus Adler and Aaron M. Margalith, *With Firmness in the Right* (New York: The American Jewish Committee, 1946), pp. 3-10.

23. For a full discussion see: Bertram W. Korn, *The American Reaction to the Mortara Case: 1858-1859* (Cincinnati: The American Jewish Archives, 1957).

24. See: Adler and Margalith, pp. 299-322.

25. *Ibid.,* pp. 99-138.

26. For an extended disucssion and chronology of American reactions see: *American Jewish Year Book 5672 (1911-1912)*, pp. 19-128; and *5673 (1912-1913)*, pp. 196-210.

27. Bertram W. Korn, *American Jewry and the Civil War* (Philadelphia: The Jewish Publication Society of America, 1957), p. 3.

28. See: Joseph Jacobs, "The Federation Movement in American Jewish Philanthropy," *American Jewish Year Book 5676 (1915-1916)*, pp. 159-198; see also Harry L. Lurie, *A Heritage Affirmed* (Philadelphia: The Jewish Publication Society of America, 1961).

29. The others were Independent Order Free Sons of Israel, Order B'nai Abraham's Order B'nai Mosche and Order Kesher Shel Barzel. See: Hyman B. Grinstein, *The Rise of the Jewish Community of New York, 1654-1860* (Philadelphia: The Jewish Publication Society, 1947).

30. For a full history see: Edward E. Grusd, *B'nai B'rith: The Story of a Covenant* (New York: Appleton-Century, 1966).

31. For a full account of the work of the JDC see: Oscar Handlin, *A Continuing Task: The American Jewish Joint Distribution Committee, 1914-1964* (New York: Random House, 1964) and Herbert Agar, *The Saving Remnant: An Account of Jewish Survival* (New York: The Viking Press, 1960).

32. Carl Wittke, *We Who Built America* (Cleveland: Case Western Reserve University Press, 1964), pp. 326-327.

33. See Selma Stern-Taeubler, "Problems of American Jewish and German Jewish Historiography," Eric D. Hirshler, editor, *Jews from Germany in the United States* (New York: Farrar, Straus and Cudahy, Inc., 1955), pp. 3-17.

34. Maldwyn Allen Jones, *American Immigration* (Chicago: The University of Chicago Press, 1960), pp. 119-120.

35. Solomon Grayzel, *A History of the Jews* (Philadelphia: The Jewish Publication Society of America, 1956), pp. 622-623.

36. Isaac Mayer Wise, *Reminiscences* (Cincinnati: Leo Wise and Co., 1901), p. 38.

37. Allan Tarshish, "The Economic Life of the American Jew in the Middle Nineteenth Century," *Essays in American-Jewish History* (Cincinnati: The American Jewish Archives, 1958), pp. 268-269.

38. Wittke, pp. 325-326.

39. For many examples see: George Cohen, *The Jews in the Making of America* (Boston: The Stratford Co., Publishers, 1924).

40. Weyl, p. 50.

41. *American Iewish Year Book 5680 (1919-1920)*, p. 598.

42. For a complete account of Jewish participation in the War Between the States and the effects of the War on the American Jewish community, see: Korn, *American Jewry and the Civil War;* also Harry Simonhoff, *Jewish Participants in the Civil War* (New York: ARCO Publishing Company, Inc., 1963).

43. Solomon Grayzel, *A History of the Jews* (Philadelphia: The Jewish Publication Society of America, 1956), pp. 622-623.

44. For a fuller biography see: Simon Wolf, "Biographical Sketch of Commodore Uriah P. Levy," *American Jewish Year Book 5663 (1902-1903)*, pp. 42-45; see also David M. Zielonka, *Introduction to a Dictionary of American Jewish Biography, 1649-1962* (Unpublished Master of Arts Thesis, Hebrew Union College-Jewish Institute of Religion, Cincinnati, 1962), pp. 218-219.

45. See: Pierce Butler, *Judah P. Benjamin* (Philadelphia: George W. Jacobs and Co., 1906).

46. *The New York Times,* June 19, 1877.

47. See John Higham, "Social Discrimination Against Jews in America, 1830-1930," reprinted from *Publication of the American Jewish Historical Society,* Vol XLVII, No. 1 (Sept., 1957). Higham points out that "discrimination can arise more or less simultaneously at every social level where a crush of applicants poses an acute problem of admission. Discrimination is probably much less a game of follow-the-leader than one of limiting the followers." (p. 11n) Vance Packard reflects the same opinion in his observation that upwardly and downwardly mobile people have a tendency to be more prejudiced in their attitude toward Jews than people who are not in motion socially. See: Vance Packard, *The Status Seekers* (New York: Pocket Books, Inc., 1961), p. 229.

48. Emanuel Gamoran, "Jewish Education in the United States,"Lotz, Philip H. and Crawford, L. W., eds, *Studies in Religious Education* (Nashville: Cokesbury Press, 1931), pp. 501-502.

49. "Sabbath Schools," *Jewish Encyclopedia* (New York: Funk and Wagnalls, 1905), Vol. X, pp. 602-603. Presently many Reform congregations are returning to the practice of *bar mitzvah.*

50. Richard C. Hertz, *The Education of the Jewish Child* (New York: Union of American Hebrew Congregations, 1953), p. 10.

51. Jacob R. Marcus, *Studies in American Jewish History* (Cincinnati: Hebrew Union College Press, 1969), p. 202.

52. See Emanuel Gamoran, "Nationalism and Religion in Jewish Education," *Jewish Education,* VII, No. 1 (January-March, 1935), 20.

53. David Philipson, *My Life as an American Jew* (Cincinnati: John G. Kidd & Son, Inc., 1951), p. 98.

54. A good account of ghetto life in Europe is found in Louis Wirth, *The Ghetto* (Chicago: University of Chicago Press, 1928), pp. 41-62.

55. See: Cronbach, p. 109.

56. For a more complete history of the Reform movement in Germany see: David Philipson, *The Reform Movement in Judaism* (New York: Macmillan Co., 1931).

57. Sylvan D. Schwartzman *Reform Judaism in the Making* (New York: Union of American Hebrew Congregations, 1962), p. 89. For a fuller account see: Charles Reznikoff and Uriah Z. Engelman, *The Jews of Charleston* (Philadelphia: The Jewish Publication Society of America, 1950), pp. 126-157. For the story of the Beth Elohim Congregation see: Lou H. Silberman, *American Impact: Judaism in the United States in the Early Nineteenth Century.* Syracuse University: The B. G. Rudolph Lectures in Judaic Studies, April 29, 1964.

58. Bernard J. Bamberger, "Introduction," *Reform Judaism: Essays by Hebrew Union College Alumni* (Cincinnati: Hebrew Union College Press, 1949), pp. 13-14.

59. For a tentative listing of German rabbis and scholars who came to America during this period see: Eric E. Hirschler, *Jews from Germany in the United States* (New York: Farrar, Straus and Cudahy, 1955), Appendix I, pp. 169-170.

60. For detailed biographical information see: Wise, *Reminiscences;* Max B. May, *Isaac Mayer Wise* (New York: G. P. Putnam's Sons, 1916); James G. Heller, *Isaac Mayer Wise: His Life, Work and Thought* (New York: The Union of American Hebrew Congregations, 1965).

61. The Americanization of Wise was due in great part to a visit he made to Washington in February, 1850. At this time Wise, serving as a rabbi in Albany, visited the New York Senator, William H. Seward. Seward arranged an introduction for Wise with President Zachary Taylor. Wise also had dinner with Daniel Webster. Wise felt much encouraged and uplifted by his visit to Washington. He stated: "My sojourn in Washington exerted an Americanizing influence upon me . . . I felt that I was one of the American people, although I had not yet been naturalized, and from that time I said 'we,' 'us,' and 'our' quite unconsciously whenever I spoke of American affairs. I felt greatly uplifted and aroused by this intercourse with the greatest spirit of the country and the kindly reception wherewith I met. The intellectual eight-day combat that I witnessed in the Senate stirred me mightily, enlarged my horizon, refreshed my mind, and taught me what was needed to become an English orator. I have never neglected an opportunity since then to go to Washington and form the acquaintance of the leading men of the nation. These have been my best teachers and my most instructive reading." See Jacob Rader

Marcus, *Memoirs of American Jews: 1775-1865,* Volume II (Philadelphia: The Jewish Publication Society of America, 1955), pp. 116-120.

62. Many of the German Jewish immigrants were doing exceptionally well in business. A number of them had become millionaires by this time. An interesting treatment of their stories may be found in: Stephen Birmingham, *Our Crowd* (New York: Dell Publishing Co., Inc., 1967).

63. Bamberger, p. 3.

64. *The American Israelite,* December 29, 1899, quoted in Bamberger, p. 15.
    A statement similar to the one made by Rabbi Isaac M. Wise was made by the eminent financier Henry Morgenthau, Sr., when he said: "We have fought our way through to liberty, equality, and fraternity ... No one shall rob us of these gains ... We Jews of America have found America to be our Zion. Therefore, I refuse to allow myself to be called a Zionist. I am an American." See Eric F. Goldman, *Rendezvous With Destiny* (New York: Random House, Inc., 1956), p. 142.

65. Bamberger, p. 15.

66. The name "Israel" is used here to mean sophisticated Jews who "really understood what Judaism is about." This was, as previously shown, a typical word usage of 19th century American Reform.

67. W. Gunther Plaut, *The Growth of Reform Judaism* (New York: World Union for Progressive Judaism, Ltd., 1965), pp. 30-31.

68. Wise's desire to unite the entire American Jewish community is reflected in the names of these organizations. Note that there is no mention of "Reform" in any of them, but rather expressed is the intention that they should become the central institutions of American Judaism.

69. David Philipson, "Judaism in American," *The Universal Jewish Encyclopedia* (New York: The Universal Jewish Encyclopedia, Inc., 1940), Vol. VI, p. 241. See also Plaut, pp. 31-41.

70. For biography see: *The Jewish Encyclopedia,* Vol. VII, pp. 662-663.

71. Note the pan-Jewish name chosen for this institution, following the pattern established by the Reform movement in the naming of its institutions.

72. For biography see: *The Jewish Encyclopedia,* Vol. VIII, pp. 679-681.

73. For biography see: *The Universal Jewish Encyclopedia* (New York: The Universal Jewish Encyclopedia, Inc., 1943), Vol. IX, pp. 393-394.

74. For a detailed history of the Conservative movement see: Moshe Davis, *The Emergence of Conservative Judaism* (Philadelphia: The Jewish Publication Society of America, 1963).

75. Note that these names are specifically Orthodox, reflecting different aspirations than those of the Reform and Conservative movements.

THE EAST EUROPEAN PERIOD

Jews in Russia - - Background

Anti-Semitism was a prominent feature of Russian culture. It was always in the minds of the Russian people, available for recall at the whim of czar or Church. And it was frequently recalled, as the czars tried to Russify the "foreign" Jewish Culture and the Church attempted to convert the "unbelievers."

A story can perhaps illustrate best the condition of the Jews in Czarist Russia.

> In the days of the Tsar, Koplinski fell off a bridge and proceeded to drown - - thrashing around and shouting for help at the top of his lungs.
>
> Two tsarist policemen heard his cries and ran to the rail, but when they saw it was a Jew in the water, they simply laughed.
>
> "Help! Help!" cried Koplinski. "I'm drowning"!
>
> "So drown, Zhid (Jew)"!
>
> And just as Koplinski started under for the proverbial third time, he had an inspiration: "Down with the Tsar"! he shouted.
>
> At once, the policemen jumped into the water, pulled Koplinski out, and arrested him for sedition.[1]

In 1794 the Pale of Settlement, which included the western part of Russia and much of Poland, was officially established by the Russian government. Because of the added residence and economic restrictions, the already precarious existence of the Jews was further undermined.

> The strict isolation in which, owing to a variety of historic causes, the Jews of the Polish Kingdom had lived for centuries was even more accentuated when Poland came under the Russian regime, for by confining the Jews to the pale of settlement and excluding them from the villages the Russian Government drove them into the congested towns and cities, in which they often formed the overwhelming majority of the population. They lived in complete segregation from their neighbors, and the non-Jews were as much a puzzle to the Jews as the latter were to the non-Jews. The terrible economic and political misery to which the Russian Jews were condemned made them look upon the whole non-Jewish population as their natural enemies, which in reality they were.[2]

Except for petty trading, small-scale farming and the few community-sponsored positions as teachers or religious functionaries, not many opportunities were available.

Czar Nicholas I (1825-1855) attempted to introduce "secular culture" and at the same time increased Jewish disabilities. His "enlightenment" was aimed at transforming the Jewish people into "Russians" and members of the Russian Orthodox Church. Part of his plan was to establish state schools, in which both Jewish and secular subjects would be taught. Because of the Jews' justified distrust, these schools failed. Further hardships were imposed by the forced conscription of eleven and twelve year old Jewish boys for 31 years of service in the Russian Army.

> ... the children were taken by force, torn away from their mothers, and amidst wailing and lamentation driven into far-off places. Many of them died of suffering and torture, and those that succeeded in completing the enormously long period of military service were rewarded at the end of it by being driven back into the pale of settlement, since, as Jews, they were not permitted to live in those very places where they had served their country.[3]

Alexander II (1855–1881) was more "liberal" than his predecessors during the early years of his reign, and the Jews of Russia were encouraged by his actions. He curbed much of the corruption which was prevalent in the Russia bureaucracy and increased opportunities for Jews to receive a secular education. Jews were generally permitted to live in the border provinces and in the city of Kiev, and a few were allowed to settle in the interior of Russia, in addition to the pale of settlement. However, this "liberal" mood did not last long. Because of active Jewish participation in the revolution in Poland (1860-1863) Alexander II restored the old system of restrictions. Privileges which had been granted during the first eight years of his reign were revoked or severly limited. When a pogrom broke out in Odessa in 1871, city officials allowed the slaughter and pillage to continue unabated for three days before they intervened. The last years of Alexander's reign brought continued oppression and poverty to the Jews of Russia.

The following years, under Alexander III (1881-1894), were even worse.

> The assassination of Tsar Alexander II in 1881 set off a wave of anti-Jewish riots and led to strict enforcement of the requirement that all Jews must reside within the Pale of Settlement, an area bordering on Germany, Austria and Rumania. A year later came the notorious May Laws, which placed restrictions upon Jewish worship, vitually debarred the Jews from agriculture, industry and the professions, excluded them from public office, and denied them educational opportunities. Persecution now became systematic, persistent and ruthless; worst of all there were the frightful pogroms of 1881-82, 1891 and 1905-06 in which countless Jews were massacred.[4]

New repressive laws were added. Military service was made more difficult, and Jews were restricted to the rank of private. At least 650 restrictive laws specifically directed against Jews were incorporated into the Russian legal system.

Mass emigration was triggered by three events: the program of Russification dogmatized by Pobiedonostsev, procurator of the Holy Synod of the Russian Orthodox Church; the May Laws decreed by Czar Alexander III; and perhaps most of all the frequent, widespread pogroms. The first two were official government policy; the pogroms were unofficial, but were strongly encouraged and usually aided by the Russia government, who found them useful for diverting the peasants from thoughts of their own misery and from hatred of the government. "Largely in consequence, Russian arrivals in the United States rose from 5,000 in 1800 to 81,000 in 1892 and then bounded upward to a peak of 258,000 in 1907."[5]

For those who did not emigrate, radicalism had a widespread appeal and won quick acceptance. Marxist Socialism seemed to offer a logical solution for an intolerable situation, and among its advocates were many Jews. The Bund, a Marxist organization of students and workers founded in 1897, served as the central agency for Jewish radicals. It "embodied all the restless social forces that had been gathering momentum in Tsarist Russia for over a generation." To achieve their goal, members of the Bund resorted to violence and sabotage when they deemed it necessary. To intimidate and destroy the Bund and other radicals, the Russian government killed or imprisoned thousands, and banished others to Siberia.[6]

Under Nicholas II (1894-1917) conditions grew even worse, Pogroms occurred regularly throughout Russia, Galicia and Roumania. Most notable was the pogrom at Kishinev on April 19-21, 1903, a blood bath that stirred the consciences of many people throughout Europe and in America. During the Russo-Japanese War of 1904-1905, large numbers of Jews were pressed into military service. Following the unsuccessful Revolution of 1905, counter-revolutionary groups conducted widespread massacres, which regularly included attacks on Jewish settlements. The "Black Duma" of 1907 added to the already great number of restrictions on Jews.

The moral and political bankruptcy of the czarist regime was demonstrated in 1911, when Mendel Beilis, a Jewish factory manager, was arrested on a charge of "ritual murder" in the death of a Russian boy. To make political capital for the czar and to make its case more dramatic, the prosecution tortured Beilis in an unsuccessful attempt to make him confess, and used bribed witnesses and falsified evidence in presenting its case. Public protest against the blatantly rigged trial included exposes in the press, denunciations by leading lawyers, protest rallies and strikes by workers. Even though the jury acquitted Beilis, Nicholas presented honors and gifts to all who had taken part in the prosecution and had "made the public aware of the Jewish menace."

At the start of World War I, Jews who were not in the army were expelled and cruelly herded out of Poland and the western provinces of Russia. Of the 600,000 expelled - - mostly women, children and the elderly - - some 100,000 starved or froze to death; and almost all of them lost their homes and businesses in the ravaging of the countryside. In 1917, faced with the German invasion and civilian and military uprisings, Nicholas II abdicated. After a short interim regime led by liberal Alexander Kerensky, Lenin and the Bolsheviks took control on November 7, 1917.

Life for the overwhelmingly anti-Bolshevik Jewish community did not improve after the Revolution, despite the fact that several Jews held important positions in the Bolshevik hierarchy. Owning property and employing workers, two things which even the smallest businessman did regularly, were crimes punishable by death. Many Jews were shot down in the streets for these "crimes," and almost all lost their livelihood. Post-war pogroms, especially in the Ukraine, took the lives of at least 70,000 Jews. The counter-revolutionary White Russian army, which equated Judaism with Bolshevism because the new government had made anti-Semitism illegal, killed some 50,000 Jews during their campaigns of 1919-21.

By the 1920's when competition and distrust between agrarians and industrial-capitalists triggered new waves of anti-Jewish propaganda - - centering ironically on purported plans by Jews to take over the world through control of capital - - most of Europe's Jewish communities were physically decimated and impoverished beyond salvation.

Immigration Statistics

During the period 1880-1933 some four million Jews left Eastern Europe. This mass emigration represented one-third of the Jews of Eastern Europe and one-fourth of all the Jews in the world. While the world Jewish population increased by more than half during these years, the number of Jews in Eastern Europe actually decreased; and the proportion of the world Jewish population dropped from 75% to 46%. Most of these emigrants came to the United States, increasing the American Jewish community from less than a quarter million to more than 3.5 million.[7]

The American Jewish community had grown slowly before 1880. In the seventeenth century, it numbered no more than 250. By the early years of national independence this had grown to probably not more than 2,500.[8] In 1818 Mordecai M. Noah estimated the Jewish population at 3,000; and in 1840 the *American Almanac* estimated 15,000. Reflecting the immigration from Germany, M.A. Berk estimated a population of 50,000 in 1840, and Wm. B. Hackenberg estimated that 230,257 lived in the United States in 1880.[9] Between 1880 and 1890, the American Jewish community quadrupled in size as some 550,000 newcomers arrived,[10] and the great years of immigration were yet to come.

In the peak years, 1899-1914, a total of 1.5 million Jews immigrated, mostly from Eastern Europe. Seven of these years saw totals of over 100,000. From 1915 to 1924, when restrictive laws virtually stopped the flow of immigrants, an additional 350,000 immigranted.[11] Unlike earlier Jewish immigration, and also unlike contemporary non-Jewish immigrant groups, the East Europeans often came in family groups rather than as individuals. For the immigration year 1925-26, for example, almost 20% were children, and 55.5% of the adults were women. The total immigration for the period 1881-1926 increased the American Jewish community by 2.3 million, a tenfold increase.[12]

In a period of just over one hundred years after M.M. Noah's estimate, the American Jewish community grew to more than one thousand times its earlier size.

The New Immigrants - - General Nature

Between 1880 and 1890 New York's Lower East Side became virtually an East European Jewish City. In 1890 the 111,690 Jews of this area constituted 69.4% of the population in the three wards near the Bowery. Of this group 11,895 (10.7%) had been in America less than two years, and Yiddish (or "Jargon," as it was then called by census-takers) was the principal language of 21,236 (19%).[13] "A well-defined Yiddish-speaking Jewish ethnic group emerged, very different in self-understanding and social conformation from the Jews of Sephardic and German origin who had preceeded them."[14]

The East European Jewish immigrant of 1880-1920 was a different kind of person than the earlier Sephardic and German immigrants. The earlier immigrants had come from countries of high cultural and economic development; the East Europeans came from nations that were backward and, in many areas, almost feudal. The earlier immigrants had come generally with a good secular education as well as a certain amount of Jewish knowledge; the East Europeans came thoroughly versed in the traditional Jewish sources, but most often with little other formal education. The earlier immigrants often moved quickly into the mainstream of American life because of their training and skills in the most modern methods of commerce and finance; the East Europeans for the most part knew only petty trading or farming and were not equipped for life in large, modern, commerce-oriented cities.

It was natural, however, that the new immigrants remained in the cities. Their life in Europe had been town-centered. In the larger cities of the Pale they maintained themselves as small traders, peddlers and artisans, or through some activity related to the religious life of the community. Even those who lived in the villages usually engaged in business activity of some kind. Some were paupers, and only a few were permitted to be workers in the large industrial centers. This urban background, although quite different from the life they faced in America, made the newly arrived Jews gravitate toward the emerging urban centers. [15] Although some 75,000 were removed to farms or smaller cities by various agencies and more than half a million voluntarily moved westward - - primarily to larger cities such as Cincinnati, Cleveland, Chicago, St. Louis, Detroit, New Orleans, Kansas City, Minneapolis and San Francisco - - about 65% remained in the major east coast port cities. By 1930 New York City held 46% of the American Jewish community (2.3 million of 5 million total); and Jews made up 30% of the total population of New York City. This made New York City the largest enclave of Jews ever to have existed, six times as large as Warsaw and five times as large as Moscow; and Philadelphia and Chicago contained Jewish communities as large as the major European centers. [16]

The Lower East Side of New York City had all the horrors of slum living; overcrowding, delapidated buildings, restless street gangs, prostitutes and pimps, unemployment and poverty. In addition, those who lived there suffered the added disability of speaking and reading only Yiddish, a language which was unfamiliar to the rest of America, even to most of their already-Americanized coreligionists. [17]

The Lower East Side was, however, unlike the ghettoes of other ethnic groups. None other was able to boast an intellectual working class, as many of the Jewish immigrants were. [18] The Yiddish newspaper *Der Tog* editorialized: "With all its faults, the East Side is the most cultured section of the entire city; the East Side is the liveliest quarter of the greatest city in America . . . The East Side is the center of lectures, debates, musical and literary evenings, etc. From the East Side libraries the greatest number of serious books are drawn. The East Side theaters have begun to play Ibsen, Hauptman, and Strindberg at the same time that Broadway amuses the people with trained dogs and horses." [19]

The intellectuals of the ghetto were an interesting mixture. The group included anarchists, socialists, and pious scholars immersed in the traditions; editors, writers and poets; playwrights and actors; and young scholars dreaming of a university education and life as a doctor or lawyer. Hutchins Hapgood described this group as the "enlightened" ones who are neither Orthodox Jews nor Americans . . . they are reactionary in their political opinions, and in matters of taste and literary ideals are Europeans rather than Americans. When they die they will leave nothing behind them, but while they live they include the most educated, forceable and talented personalities of the quarter.[20]

The masses of immigrants who settled in the rapidly changing centers of industrializing America faced many problems in adapting to their new homeland.

Everything in the new environment, the radically different standards and ideals of a highly industrialized community, the political freedom, the utterly different attitude of the neighboring population, the demands of general education which characteristically enough the Russian Jew immediately accepted as a matter of course . . . and, at the top, and perhaps at the bottom of it all, the fierce economic struggle of the newcomers with the infinitely greater prospects of success which it held forth for them - - all these circumstances were equally bound to revolutionize their time-honored ideas and ideals.[21]

Despite the economic, linguistic and educational disabilities which the new immigrants faced, they - - and especially their children - - were singularly successful in acculturating. They emphasized working hard, making the most of opportunities and, especially, securing the best possible education for their children. "By being Jewish they were, in a very curious way, becoming more typically American . . . paradoxically the most 'American' of all the ethnic groups that went into the making of modern America."[22]

Efforts to Aid the Immigrants

The American Jewish community was not prepared for the masses of new immigrants who suddenly began to arrive. They had neither the numbers to absorb them nor the wealth to support that many newcomers. In 1880 Jews were 0.6% of the total population of the United States; by 1917 they were 3.5%[23] They had, in fact, resisted the request for greatly increased immigration made by European relief agencies for ten years, and in 1882 sent a delegation to a meeting of the United European relief agencies to work for an end to immigration from Eastern Europe into the United States.[24] Partly this reaction was from ignorance of the real situation in Europe. Few detailed reports came to them in the American or Anglo-Jewish press at this time, and those who read the European press usually knew of only the events reported in the German newspapers. Partly, however, their actions reflected the embarassment which they, as already-Americanized citizens, felt at the strange manners and uncouth ways of the unsophisticated newcomers. Isaac Mayer Wise, in an editorial on September 26, 1884, presented a representative American position.

> It is not only the *Jewish World* of London which expects from the influx of Russian and Roumanian Jews in the United States a retrogression of Judaism to the medieval and demi-cabalistic standard of the "Shulchan Aruch," but there are quite a number of very intelligent gentlemen in our country who apprehend similar results for the religious and social standing of American Israelites by the influx of an element so entirely foreign, and in many cases, entirely outlandish. This apprehension makes of them opponents of immigration . . . It is expected that the Jew be a decent, clean, civilized man, who submits gracefully to sanitary laws and police regulations, uses soap, and dresses like other people, which we hear is not the case with all those new-comers, for a good long while. This may produce and intensify social prejudices against our co-religionists at least for the time being, and ought to be counteracted by charitable people everywhere. Persuade them not to establish new Ghettoes for themselves, not to live together in one narrow quarter, to send their children to public schools, to use more soap and less "Schulchan Aruch." . . .
> Let them come by the thousands, we are not afraid of them; we welcome them as friends and brothers, and are willing to assist them wherever we can.[25]

Despite these reservations, as the flood of immigrants grew, the native and Americanized Jewish community rose to the challenge of helping them.

The United Hebrew Charities of New York City, founded in 1874, increased its activities to provide food, lodging and medical services. Its employment bureau had notable success in placing the untrained immigrants in jobs. The National Council of Jewish Women, founded in 1893, undertook to protect the interests of immigrant girls. The Union of American Hebrew Congregations and B'nai B'rith provided many services in the mid-west, south and south-west.

The Industrial Removal Office, founded in 1901 by wealthy "Germans" to break up immigrant enclaves and route them out of New York City, removed some 60,000 into smaller communities, mostly in the midwest. However, this was not fast enough to keep up with the influx of East Europeans. Since the new immigrants were arriving so rapidly and were reluctant to leave their port of entry, the Galveston Plan was devised. Immigrants were persuaded before they left Europe to enter the United States at Galveston, Texas, rather than New York. Beginning in 1907, the plan operated rather successfully until it was interrupted by World War I.

One of the great sources of assistance was the Baron de Hirsch Fund, endowed by an original grant of $2,400,000 from Baron Maurice de Hirsch, a German industrialist and philanthropist. Incorporated in 1891 with "Germans" as its officers and directors, The Fund gave immediate assistance to new immigrants and later provided job training for both light industry and agriculture. One of its major efforts was the establishment of agricultural colonies. The Fund often worked in cooperation with the United Hebrew Charities and with the Jewish Colonization Association (ICA), which also had been funded by Baron de Hirsch.

By no means should one assume that the immigrants did nothing to help themselves. Partly because they resented the patronizing way in which the "Germans" provided aid and rushed them into "Americanizing" at the expense of familiar habits and manners, and partly because it was their religious duty to help their co-religionists, the new immigrants established a wide range of self-help organizations as soon as they were able to do so. In the 1880's the many *landsmanschaften*[26] provided life insurance, sick benefits, interest free loans and the assistance of a burial society. By 1914 there were over five hundred *landsmanschaften* which included in their membership almost the entire Jewish immigrant population of New York City.

As early as 1892 Russian immigrants started the Hebrew Free Loan Society, whose primary purpose was to loan a few dollars, interest free, to newly arrived immigrants who wanted to become independent businessmen. The loans, usually about ten dollars, were enough to stock a peddler's basket of soft goods and start men on their new careers.

The founders of the Hebrew Immigrant Aid Society were mostly Hungarian immigrants and members of the Independent Order of B'rith Abraham. This society, which received almost $200,000 in contributions from both Jews and non-Jews in America and an additional $100,000 in Europe during its first year, provided a wide range of services. Its members served as interpreters and as voluntary attorneys to protect immigrants from the misinterpretation of laws or the misuse of discretionary powers by immigration workers. They located the families of new immigrants, ran an employment service and maintained a temporary shelter house in New York City.

Although their efforts duplicated many existing agencies, the new immigrants founded and operated hospitals, orphanages, old-age homes, burial societies, travelers aid societies, and societies to aid families, widows, children, the deaf, prisoners and unwed mothers. In all of these organizations the new immigrants could feel "at home" and not patronized, and they worked hard to expand these self-help services.

Agricultural Colonies

One of the ideals of the Haskala (Enlightenment) was the "normalization" of Jewish life through a return to agriculture, an occupation from which Jews were generally excluded in Eastern Europe. Many of the younger immigrants, influenced by the *Haskala,* "entertained fantastic notions about the virtue of agriculture" and eagerly "fell in with all colonization plans, for which they had more enthusiasm than natural aptitude."[27]

Among the most active proponents of agricultural colonization was Michael Heilprin. He had been active in liberal causes in Hungary before emigrating to America, and soon after his arrival in 1856 he became an active and vocal abolitionist. Among his many efforts on behalf of the new immigrants, he sponsored agricultural colonies and encouraged the newcomers to become farmers.[28]

Most of the agricultural colonies founded in America were sponsored by the Baron de Hirsch Fund, the Jewish Agricultural Society and the Jewish Colonization Association. Over a period of years some three thousand families were settled in such towns as Woodbine and Alliance, New Jersey, and on farms in Connecticut, New York and New Jersey. Smaller, less successful colonies were started at Sicily Island, Catahoula Parish, Louisiana; Cremieux and Betlehem Yehudah Colony, Davison County, South Dakota; and in Oregon, Colorado, Virginia, Michigan and Kansas.[29]

Economics Introduction

By the time Jews began arriving in large numbers from Eastern Europe, many of the economic frontiers that had been open to their German predecessors no longer existed. The development of the department store and reliable mail order companies had minimized the role of both city and rural peddlers. Increased use of the sewing machine in the garment and shoe industries virtually eliminated the used clothing business, which had been a major industry and lucrative field of opportunity before the Civil War. Although the frontier was not officially declared closed until after the 1890 census,[30] as far as the East European Jew was concerned, it held no promise even before that.

The East European Jewish immigrants arrived at a booming period of industrialization and urbanization, and they soon filled the unskilled and semi-skilled positions in various American industries. The garment industry, especially, and also the cigar making and household supplies industries called for the help of cheap immigrant labor; and the new immigrants were willing to accept almost any wage. It was in the light industries to which the immigrants were attracted that Jewish labor leaders got their start, and in the sweatshop the immigrants received their indoctrination in the American ways of business.

Though impoverished like other immigrant groups, the Jewish working class remained unique. Despite their initial poverty and strangeness, they "had the effects of two thousand year old experience as merchants and scholars. They had broader horizons than the working class of other groups."[31]

The Jewish blue collar worker was, for the most part, a one-generation phenomenon. "The 'deproletarianization' of the Jewish immigrant began almost as soon as he became proletarianized."[32] Like all Americans, the East European Jewish immigrants strove for social and economic advancement. Unlike most immigrants, they were overwhelmingly successful in reaching their goal. Some moved upward from the working class during the first generation; by the second generation most were in the professions or white collar occupations.

The Needle Trades and the Jewish Labor Movement

The use of the sewing machine revolutionized the production of all types of clothing. Tailored clothing, individually fitted by highly skilled craftsmen for a select clientèle gave way to ready-made clothing, mass produced by semi-skilled machine operators for the public-at-large. The immigrant tailor who learned his trade through a long apprenticeship and practiced it alone in his shop was now able to take home large quantities of machine-cut patterns for his wife, children or relatives to stitch in place. By 1900, between 150,000 and 200,000 Jewish immigrants and their families - - a total of almost one million people - - depended on the needle trades for their livelihood.[33]

This piecework approach to production, in addition to the social revolution it created by making it possible for every man and woman to dress fashionably, in new clothes, brought about the recognition of three distinct grades of clothing. The superior grade was still made by a master tailor. The second grade was measured and cut by a master, but was assembled by a worker in his home, often with the help of his family. The lowest grade was cut in quantity from a standard pattern and distributed to contractors, who either farmed out the work to be done in various workers' homes or maintained a workshop in their own homes. As the clothing industry achieved a place of prominence in American business, it became increasingly dominated by the third method of production.

It was from this approach, in which the manufacturer provided only the designing of the garments and the cutting of the cloth, and the contractor provided capital, handled all of the technical processes and hired the necessary labor, that the infamous "sweatshop" evolved. Contractors bid competitively for the job of assembling the pre-cut bundles and could make a profit only by demanding from their workers long hours at low wages.

The workers in the sweatshops worked in crowded, unsanitary conditions and received the lowest possible wages. A sixteen-hour working day was not uncommon, with the pay scale usually ranging from six to ten dollars a week for men and half that for women.

Interest in the labor union movement grew slowly among the first generation immigrants. Scattered attempts at organization had been made prior to 1890, but they were generally ineffective. There were many obstacles to overcome: workers often were employed by a *landsman* (a person from the same town in the old country), and they trusted him to treat them fairly; the industry itself was undeveloped and disorganized (a new company could be started with less than $100 capital); the mass of semi-skilled workers lacked the tradition of being working class people, and were not subject to the usual appeals of union organizers; the workers were often Orthodox Jews, and they distrusted the radical, atheistic approach of many labor leaders; and the surplus of immigrant workers made it easy for a contractor to replace any worker who showed an interest in the unions.

The United Hebrew Trades, founded in 1888, grew to a membership of almost six thousand in its first two years. Morris Hillquit was its first secretary, and his correspondence, which he conducted in Yiddish, stressed Jewish loyalty as much as Socialist ideals. Daniel de Leon, president of UHT and a doctrinaire revolutionary Socialist, led the membership into a series of violent, unproductive strikes during the 1890's during which the workers came to realize that he was more interested in communizing American society than in winning practical benefits for his followers. By 1900 the UHT was reduced to one-tenth of its earlier strength; and Jewish workers after this experience refused to follow radical leaders, although their interest in socialism never waned.

> The most articulate and one of the most important centers of Socialism was New York City, particularly lower Manhattan. Union Square and the garment district had bred socialism even before there was a Socialist Party. Here in earlier years had been the main strength of the Socialist Labor Party, and when De Leon's personality and policies had brought revolt within his party most of his former followers went into the Socialist Party. The rank and file of the New York movement were immigrants, largely Jewish needle trade workers from eastern Europe. To these hard-working people Socialism was more than just a

political movement; it was a way of life. In some neighborhoods one grew up to be a Socialist, a reader of Abraham Cahan's *Jewish Daily Forward,* in Yiddish, or the *Call,* in English, and a member of one of the needle trade unions just as naturally as in some other parts of the country one grew up to be a Republican and a reader of the *Saturday Evening Post.*[34]

Between 1900 and the outbreak of World War I four "Jewish" unions were formed: the International Ladies' Garment Workers Union (1900), which represented most of the employees in the women's garment industry by 1910; the Cap Maker's Union (1901); the Fur Workers' Union (1904); and the Amalgamated Clothing Workers' Union (1914). These unions proved to be stable and powerful. They were able not only to achieve the goals of all unions - - shorter hours, higher wages and better working conditions - - but also to pioneer in the areas of labor-management relations and union-provided services to their members.

Public sympathy for the plight of the workers was aroused especially by two events. In 1901 the ILGWU led a strike of waist and dress makers, known as "the uprising of the twenty thousand;" and in March, 1911, a fire at the Triangle Shirt Waist Company of New York took the lives of 146 workers who were trapped inside the building.

The critical event, however, was a general strike in 1910, in which 60,000 garment workers left their jobs and paralyzed the entire industry. Because of the bitterness and violence of the conflict and the "bad publicity" it engendered (both labor and management were Jewish), leaders of the Jewish community formed a mediation board and through the efforts of Louis Marshall, Jacob H. Schiff and, especially, Louis D. Brandeis drafted a "protocol of peace." This settlement ended the sweatshop by eliminating piecework labor in both the workers' and the contractors' homes; setting shorter hours, higher wages and improved working conditions; forming a labor-management board of health; and establishing a permanent arbitration board, made up of representatives of labor, management and the public, to settle future disputes. Because it firmly established the principle of collective bargaining, this was one of the most important events in the history of the American labor movement.

For the most part, these unions have maintained the policies and operating principles with which they started. During the 1920's supporters of communism made some inroads in the New York locals; however, they never controlled more than a small portion of the unions' memberships. A strike in which the leaders refused to negotiate with management disillusioned many union members; and the appeals of Al Smith and Franklin D. Roosevelt drew many into the ranks of liberalism and the Democratic Party by the 1930's.

Journalism

The language of the East European Jewish immigrant was Yiddish, a folk jargon of German, Hebrew, Aramaic and whatever language was spoken in the area in which the Jews resided. Because of its flexibility, Yiddish quickly incorporated many English words and phrases; and English, in turn, has adopted much of the Yiddish idiom.[35]

The earliest Yiddish writings in America were self-consciously slow to absorb the American idiom. However, by the 1890's the Yiddish press reflected an Americanized Yiddish, often using English words spelled phonetically in the Hebrew alphabet. "Matching [Alexander] Harkavy's exertion [in Yiddish lexicography], fellow Lithuanians Abraham Cahan and George Selikowitch gave literary currency to the spoken Lithuanian idiom. Yet these pioneer journalists placed small stock in the vernacular's literary capacity, viewing Yiddish as no more than a makeshift on the road to Americanization and modernization." [36]

Abraham Cahan, writing in the *Atlantic Monthly* in July, 1898, noted the momentary importance of Yiddish publications for the Americanization of the new immigrants.

> The innumerable Yiddish publications with which the Jewish quarter is flooded are also a potent civilizing and Americanizing agency. The Russian Jews of New York, Philadelphia and Chicago have within the last twenty years created a vast periodical literature which furnishes intellectual food not only to themselves but also to their brethren in Europe. A feverish literary activity unknown among the Jews of Russia, Roumania, and Austria, but which has arisen here among the immigrants from those countries, educates thousands of ignorant tailors and peddlers, lifts their intelligence, facilitates their study of English, and opens to them the doors of the English library . . . The Yiddish periodicals are so many preparatory schools from which the reader is sooner or later promoted to the English newspaper, just as the several Jewish theatres prepare his way to the Broadway playhouse, or as the Yiddish lecture serves him as a stepping-stone to that English-speaking self-educational society, composed of workingmen who have lived a few years in the country, which is another characteristic feature of life in the Ghetto. Truly, the Jews "do not rot in their slum, but, rising, pull it up after them." [37]

The first Yiddish periodical to appear in America was the *Yiddishe Zeitung* (1870), which drew its material from German-

and Hebrew-language periodicals of Europe. With the exception of the *Yiddishe Gazetten,* which was published from 1874 to 1928, all attempts to start a Yiddish press in the 1870's failed.

Increased immigration after 1880, and especially in the 1890's, accompanied by a drastic reduction in the price of newsprint and the adoption of linotype printing, made a daily press possible. Between 1885 and 1914, more than 150 Yiddish language journals, periodicals and newspapers appeared.[38]

The most influential and successful of the Yiddish journalists was Abraham Cahan, editor of the *Vorwartz, (The Jewish Daily Forward)* from 1902 to 1951. Cahan came to America in 1882 as an ambitious twenty one year old. Although he worked as a factory laborer, lecturer, teacher of English, labor organizer, law student and socialist preacher, his first love and greatest ambition was journalism. During his first year in America Cahan authored an article for the *New York World* describing the coronation of Czar Alexander III. Within a few years his work included both writing for and editing Russian, Yiddish and English periodicals. Through his friendship with Lincoln Steffens, he was hired to write human interest features and character sketches for the *New York Sun,* the *New York Evening Post* and the *New York Commercial Advertiser.* When Steffens became city editor of the *Commercial Advertiser,* he engaged Cahan as a regular staff member.

In 1902 Cahan became editor of the *Vorwartz.* Almost singlehandedly he built it from a sectarian journal with less than 6,000 readers into a modern newspaper with a daily circulation of almost a quarter of a million.[39]

The *Vorvartz* supported moderate, pragmatic socialism, the working man and humanity. Its great appeal to its readers was the prominent role of human interest features and columns. One of the most popular was "Bintel Brief" (Bundle of Letters), a letters-to-the-editor column in which the readers asked advice in solving both personal and religious problems. The answers given combined social work and advice-to-the lovelorn into a primer on Americanization. Cahan also published such Americanizating articles as English lessons, reports of Congressional debates, episodes of American history, problems of current American life, and a 1909 explanation of "The Fundamentals of Baseball Explained to Non-Sports," which included a three-column diagram of the Polo Grounds.[40]

Over the years Cahan became increasingly conservative and less interested in socialism and the Socialist Movement.[41] In 1933 he was expelled from the Socialist Party because of his supporting Franklin D. Roosevelt and the New Deal. He was also among the earliest opponents of communism.

Abe Cahan was among the first political journalists in America to recognize that communism was a threat to democratic institutions. He saw this even before the Bolshevik revolution and remained consistent in his opposition for the rest of his life. In the early 1930's, he secured credentials from Senator William Borah to send his Sunday editor, Harry Lang, on a trip to Russia. When Lang began his series of articles on the totalitarianism of the Soviet Union, and the articles were translated in the New York Evening Journal, many uptown conservatives called these old social-democrats "red-baiters," and the communists burned Cahan and Lang in effigy in Union Square.[42]

The Yiddish Theatre

One of the few amusements available in the East Side Jewish community was the Yiddish Theatre. Operating seven days a week, including the Sabbath, the many theatrical companies presented a wide variety of plays. Actors and playwrights were held in esteem bordering on veneration by their followers, and attendance at all the theatres averaged over five thousand for each of the nine performances each week.

Musicals and operettas were particularly popular, and the sheet music for favorite songs was sold in many of the bookstores. Other plays, particularly popular with first generation immigrants, were "culture pieces," picturing in melodramatic terms the persecution of Jews by Christians or the disillusionment of devout older-generation parents with their agnostic, rebellious children. Romanticized and Judaized adaptations of the plays of Shakespeare, Schiller, Hauptmann and others - - hardly identifiable with the original versions of any of them - - were much in demand among the intellectuals. "In almost every play given on the Bowery all the elements are represented. Vaudeville, history, realism, comic opera, are generally mixed together."[43]

Abraham Cahan held the view that the Yiddish theatre offered little of value but was still important.

The playwrights pay very little attention to language, characterization and to a true depiction of Jewish life ... The main aim of the playwrights and promoters is to attract the masses and sell tickets ... Notwithstanding the low literary standard, the plays amuse the public and bring a little variety into the monotonous life of the Russian-Jewish immigrant.[44]

Because the Yiddish Theatre was so popular, it was a major cultural force in the ghetto. By introducing American-style musical and dramatic plays, dramatizing American life and the problems it posed for the immigrants and portraying life in a vocabulary that was rich in Americanisms, the Yiddish theatre both amused and educated the inhabitants of the East Side.

Education – Introduction

One of the reasons for the great migration was the dearth of secular educational opportunities in Europe.

Within the Jewish community there were ample opportunities to study the traditions. Even the smallest communities considered it a point of honor to have a school and a resident teacher. Larger communities usually maintained both elementary and advanced schools.[45] Throughout the nineteenth century Jewish students from all over Europe flocked to the celebrated academies of Eastern Europe, where they could obtain a Jewish education of outstanding quality.

However, the secular schools and universities were virtually closed to Jewish students.

> General secular education was at a low ebb in Russia; it was certainly far inferior both in extent and intensity to Jewish educational requirements. Yet even these meager educational advantages were withheld from the Jews; and when in a whim of despotic generosity . . . the Russian government decided . . . to drag the Jews to secular education, it was suspected by them as an effort to land the Russian Jews in the fold of the Greek Orthodox Church. No wonder, therefore, that the Jews anxiously shunned all general education and lived their own life. They spoke their own language (Yiddish); and wore their own dress, and were in every manifestation of life Jews, nothing but Jews.[46]

Jewish youth, raised in a tradition which stressed the value of education, saw university training as the way to obtain higher status in Russian society and a professional degree as a passport into the world-at-large. By the 1880's, however, Jews were almost completely barred from Russian and Polish institutions of higher learning, and Jewish intellectuals were forced to abandon hope for professional advancement. Some studied at the universities of Switzerland and Germany where, caught between a bleak past and a hopeless future, they became disciples of socialism or, more frequently, Marxist revolutionism.

Others lost faith in the possibility of improving life in Eastern Europe and emigrated to America. In the United States their zest for education was expressed in three major ways: the establishment of schools for the religious education of their children; the development of adult study courses, lecture series and literary societies; and, most of all, support of the public school system and institutions of higher learning, and the insistence that their children remain in these schools as long as possible.

Classes for the Children

The knowledge of some Hebrew prayers, a little history and the Five Books of Moses in English, which was roughly the objective of the Reform Sunday Schools of this time, would not have been enough to save the East European Jew from being called an *am-haaretz* (ignoramus). The education of the East European Jew was instruction in a total culture which was rooted in the Torah and the Talmud. The ability to understand a Talmudic text, which took years of study, was the minimum requirement for anyone who wished his religious opinions to be of any consequence in the Jewish community.[47]

At first the Russian immigrants tried to recreate the educational system they had known in the pale of settlement. The *heder* and the *yeshiva* were the only schools in which the East Europeans could have confidence,[48] and the education these schools provided had been necessary for their way of life there. The attempts made at this time were not the first try at establishing all-day Jewish schools in America. Several "German" congregations had done so a generation earlier. None of the attempts, however, met with much success.[49]

The attempts to create European-style all-day schools failed basically for three reasons: the schools as established were generally of low quality; as the Russian immigrants became Americanized there was a widespread feeling that this kind of education was not really necessary for their new life; and the free public schools were readily available, and the realities of American life made a good secular education imperative for social advancement.

The schools that were established were continually under-financed. The principal of a school might earn $8 to $12 a week (when he was paid), and teachers earned about $4.[50] Because Hebrew teachers in the United States were often men who were too old or too weak to work in a factory or operate a business, because they seldom had any training in pedagogy and because they often had neither the personality or the knowledge to be effective teachers, Hebrew teachers were among the least respected members of the community.[51]

Alexander M. Dushkin, former director of the Bureau of Jewish Education of New York City, recalled his family's early days in America: "There [in New York] my father tried to follow his profession of Jewish teaching, but in those days the lot of the American Hebrew teacher was so degrading and so hopeless that he could not endure it."[52] Hutchins Hapgood echoed this sentiment when he described the Jewish scholar and teacher in America as a beggar living in poverty.

[He is] unknown and unhonored, for he has pinned his

63

faith to a declining cause . . . and consequently amid the
crowding and material interests of the new world he is
submerged - - poor in physical estate and his moral capital
unrecognized by the people among whom he lived.[53]

In the American society to which the new immigrants were
adapting, religion played a secondary role. Unlike the pale of
settlement, the ghetto or the shtetl, where religious and civil law
were virtually synonymous, religion in America functioned mostly
after business hours and on weekends and holidays. Especially for
members of a minority religious group who were eager to
acculturate, the knowledge of the fine points of religious law grew
increasingly less important. For the new immigrant, and especially
in the dreams which the new immigrant had for his children, the
study of secular subjects in English was far more important than
the study of religious subjects in Hebrew or Yiddish.

The public school had already been accepted as the prime
educational agency for all children before the East Europeans
arrived. The principle of "common schools," available to all
children without regard to social class and free of any cost was a
uniquely American idea. By 1860 public education was part of
American life in all the urban centers.[54]

The new immigrants accepted the public schools with great
enthusiasm, quite often at the expense of Jewish religious
education.[55] Dr. Samson Benderly, Director of the Bureau of
Education of the Jewish Community of New York, estimated that
for the year 1910-1911 only one fourth of the 200,000 Jewish
children of school age received any kind of religious instruction. [56]
Almost all of these children, however, were enrolled in the public
schools. Parents were convinced that the public schools were the
vehicle for integration into American society and out of the
sweatshop. "Jews . . .perhaps more than any other immigrant
group, cherished the public schools as a vehicle of Americanization
and advancement in American life."[57]

The same pattern was discerniable in colleges and universities. A
survey conducted in 1908 of seventy seven institutions of higher
learning showed that 8.5% of the students were first and second
generation Jewish immigrants. In schools of pharmacy there were
18%, and in schools of law 13%. These figures were particularly
noteworthy because Jews made up only 2% of the total
population at this time.[58]

Under these conditions, the Jewish schools could not succeed
without changing and giving ground. "The long hours of study
which were an indispensable condition of their success in Russia
are impossible in this country, in which the public school claims
the best time and energy of the child."[59] Although some all-day
schools did start and have continued, for the most part the day

school movement has been unsuccessful. Even today such schools in most cities depend on community support to stay open. In response to this situation, Jewish schools took on a new direction peculiar to America.

The religious education of most Jewish children was limited to attendance at the after-school sessions of a Talmud Torah or the weekly classes of a Sunday School. While the Sunday Schools, which were usually affiliated with a Reform congregation, stressed Bible study in English, Jewish history, religion and customs, and a smattering of Hebrew,[60] the Talmud Torah stressed the study of the Hebrew language, Biblical and rabbinic texts in Hebrew, and the *siddur* (traditional prayer book). The curriculum of the American Talmud Torah was essentially the same as that of a European *heder,* but reduced to an after-school schedule. It differed from its European counterpart only in the amount of study time and correspondingly in the amount accomplished.[61]

In addition to these schools, attempts were made to establish schools which would present specific points of view. As early as the 1890's there were Zionist-oriented schools which stressed Jewish nationalism and the use of Hebrew as a spoken language. By 1910 Yiddish-language schools existed in several cities, and Socialist-oriented Sunday Schools had been opened and closed. During the decade before World War I teachers and writers imbued with the education ideals of the *Haskala* and Hebrew-Renaissance movements came to America. These men worked to develop a Hebrew-cultural heritage by the use of new approaches to education. They opened a few private schools, and established the National Hebrew Schools and supplementary week-day schools. In S. H. Neumann's private school in Brooklyn, for example, Hebrew was taught as a living language, attempts were made to group students by age, and modern teaching techniques were utilized.[62] The curriculum of the National Hebrew School in Manhattan and the Hebrew National School for Girls in Brooklyn emphasized the Hebrew language and the study of Zionism. In addition, Dr. Samson Benderly conducted an experimental Hebrew school in Baltimore, and Rabbi Morris Levine was instrumental in establishing the Hebrew Institute in Chicago.[63]

In order to further Jewish interests in New York City and to solve some of the enormous problems that the Jews of that city faced, leaders of various Jewish groups met in 1909. Under the leadership of Dr. Judah L. Magnus, one of the outstanding leaders of the American Zionist movement and a noted Reform rabbi, this group set about forming a *Kehillah.*[64] The Kehillah set up courts of arbitration, a welfare bureau and a Bureau of Jewish Education. Within a few years the Kehillah failed because it had no authority to enforce its decisions and internal frictions weakened it. The only lasting result of the Kehillah was the Bureau of Jewish Education. Under the leadership of its first director, Dr. Samson Benderly, a physican who surrendered his practice to devote his efforts to the improvement of Jewish religious education, the Bureau developed into a potent force for the improvement of Talmud Torahs and Hebrew schools.[65]

Benderly's influence extended beyond the work of the Bureau because of his disciples. He brought together and trained a group of outstanding young educators to continue his work. Among the teachers of this group were Benderly, Magnus, Israel Friedlaender, chairman of the Bureau's Board of Trustees and a leader of the Zionist movement, and Mordecai M. Kaplan, professor at the Jewish Theological Seminary and founder of the Reconstructionist movement. Within this group arose a drive for the popularization of Jewish education among both children and adults. In addition to their work, with Hebrew schools and Sunday Schools, they pioneered in the field of modern adult education. In 1919, under the sponsorship of the Jewish Theological Seminary, the Israel Friedlaender classes for the popularization of Jewish knowledge among adults were created. Based on the pattern of these classes, a number of institutes and academies were founded by individual congregations and Jewish Community Centers throughout the country.

Programs for the Adults

Social and literary clubs already existed in the United States when the East European immigrants arrived, though they usually had little specifically Jewish content. The earliest of these had been founded in the 1840's by German Jewish immigrants, and in the 1850's these clubs had banded together as the Young Men's Hebrew Association (YMHA). These YMHA's and the Young Women's Hebrew Association (YWHA), which was founded shortly after this, served as community centers for the new immigrants. They offered dances, plays and athletics for the young people, as well as lectures and schooling in Jewish studies. Often the "Y" provided the only Jewish library and reading room in a neighborhood, and in many cases it housed a Talmud Torah or a Sunday School for the children of poor families.

One of the most important parts of its program was a broad spectrum of Americanization courses. This, as far as the already-Americanized "Germans" and the anxious-to-Americanize "Russians" were concerned, was probably its most valuable function. The newcomers in most cases participated eagerly in such programs as English classes, lectures in English or Yiddish on current American problems or on American history, citizenship classes and special classes to acquaint the new immigrant with

66

American mores.[66]   The Educational Alliance, built in the heart of the Lower East Side, was established in 1889 to further these programs; and it was soon imitated in other major settlements.[67] The program of the Hebrew Free School Association included classes in industrial arts and social amenities; and the National Federation of Temple Sisterhoods, starting with Temple Emanuel Sisterhood of New York, sponsored similar classes and maintained day care centers.[68]

Settlement houses were started and maintained by sympathetic American social reformers such as Lillian D. Wald (Henry Street Settlement in New York City) and Jane Addams (Hull House in Chicago). The program of these settlement houses included family and personal counselling, programs to combat juvenile delinquency, the giving of food and clothing to needy families, and training the immigrants in the ways of their new country. Because those who ran the settlement houses were the first social workers who lived with the immigrants in the midst of the slums, they were liked, respected and trusted by those whom they were trying to help. And because they knew first hand the problems that the new immigrants faced, they could effectively help the immigrants solve their problems.

Social services such as these were very valuable in helping to soften the impact of adjustment to a harsh and alien society.

Synagogues

Until the 1880's most of the East European immigrants joined the Sephardic or German congregations which already existed. As early at 1762 a Luthuanian Jew, Abraham son of R. Isaac Brisker, was in the employ of the Sephardic Congregation Shearith Israel of New York.[69]   As the number of East Europeans rose,[70] however, they were no longer willing to submit to the religious domination of either the Sephardim or the Germans.

In 1852 Russian immigrants joined together to form the Beth Hamidrash (later known as Beth Hamidrash Hagodol — "The Great Synagogue") with Abraham Joseph Ash as its rabbi. Here the Russian pronunciation of Hebrew (as distinct from Sephardic or German pronunciation) was used, and the service was conducted in accordance with the minutiae of Russian-Jewish customs.[71]   When the great waves of immigration began, members of Beth Hamidrash Hagodol took an active role in providing relief; and the congregation served for a while as the "mother church" for the many small congregations which sprung up all over the lower East Side.

The number of congregations rose rapidly during this period. Whereas in 1854 there were fourteen synagogues (including both

67

orthodox and reform), only one of which was specifically Russian, by 1890 the number had grown to one hundred fifty and by 1900 to more than three hundred.[72] Most of these new congregations were very small, often no larger than a *minyan* (the quorum of ten men required for a worship service), and very poor. Few had rabbis or cantors except on the most important holidays, and the daily and Sabbath services were conducted by members of the congregation during the rest of the year. The day-to-day operation of the congregation was supervised by the, *shammos* (beadle), who often served also as the Hebrew School teacher. Most commonly the membership consisted of families who had come from the same town or were members of the same synagogue in the old country.

In 1888 Rabbi Jacob Joseph of Vilna was brought to New York to head a proposed *kehillah* of the orthodox community. Despite his reputation as a rabbinic authority and the efforts put forth to organize the kehillah, the plan failed. Congregations, organizations and independent religious functionaries were unwilling to surrender their independence and submit to community discipline. A similar attempt made fifteen years later in Chicago also failed.

Voluntarism was too much a part of the American religious picture to be overcome by anyone's plan for community organization.

FOOTNOTES

For the East European Period

1. Leo Rosten, *The Joys of Yiddish* (New York: Pocket Books, 1970), p. 438.
2. Israel Friedlaender, "The Problem of Jewish Education in America and the Bureau of Education of the Jewish Community of New York City," *Report of the Commissioner of Education for the New Year Ended June 30, 1913.* Vol. 1, (Washington, D.C.; U. S. Government Printing Office, 1913), p. 369
3. Emanuel Gamoran, *Changing Conceptions in Jewish Education,* Book I, (New York: The Macmillian Company, 1924), p. 33.
4. Maldwyn Allen Jones, *American Immigration* (Chicago: University of Chicago Press, 1960), pp. 201-02.
55. *Ibid.,* p. 202
6. Moses Rischin, *The Promised City* (Cambridge, Mass.: Harvard University Press, 1962), pp. 10, 42.
7. See: Ismar Elbogen, *A Century of Jewish Life,* trans. Moses Hadas (Philadelphia: The Jewish Publication Society of America, 1944), pp. 326-336; also Howard Morely Sachar, *The Course of Modern Jewish History* (New York: Delta Books of Dell Publishing Co., Inc., 1958), pp. 306-315
8. Jacob Rader Marcus, *Early American Jewry* (Philadelphia: The Jewish Publication Society of America, 1955), Vol. II, p. 393.
9. *The American Jewish Year Book, 5660 (1899-1900)* (Philadelphia: The Jewish Publication Society of America, 1899), p. 283.
10. *Ibid.,* pp. 283-284
11. "Migrations of the Jews," *The Universal Jewish Encyclopedia,* ed. Isaac Landman (New York: The Universal Jewish Encyclopedia, Inc., 1942), Vol. VII, pp. 548-549.
12. *The American Jewish Year Book, 5688 (1927-1928),* p. 250-258.
13. Figures are from the Eleventh United States Census, 1890, cited in: Lloyd P. Gartner, "The Jews of New York's East Side, 1890-1893, *"American Jewish Historical Quarterly* (New York: American Jewish Historical Society, 1964), Vol. LIII, No. 3 (March, 1964), pp. 268-270.
14. Will Herberg, *Protestant-Catholic-Jew: An Essay in American Religious Sociology* (Garden City, New York: Anchor Books of Doubleday and Company, Inc., 1960), p. 179.
15. Ellis Rivkin, "A Decisive Pattern in American Jewish History," in *Essays in American Jewish History* (Cincinnati: The American Jewish Archives, 1958), p. 40. Dr. Rivkin's thesis receives some support from Gilbert Osofsky, who points to this urban orientation and experience in relation to property buying and moving "uptown" from the Lower East Side to Harlem, in *Harlem: The Making of a Ghetto* (New York: Harper and Row, Publishers, 1968), esp. pp. 87-88.
16. See: Elbogen, pp. 428-429, and Sachar, pp. 316-317.
17. It should be noted that other immigrants spoke a "national" language - - English, Spanish, German, Italian, Polish, Russian and so forth - - which they shared with fellow nationals of all religions. Yiddish, or Judeo-German, was a jargon particular to the Jews of Eastern Europe. While it was based on German, it existed in many dialects because of the addition of words from the various East European languages spoken by the residents of the areas in which the Jews lived. Although more than three-fourths of the immigrants were literate (an unusually high literacy rate), their knowledge enabled them to communicate only with each other and initially created a social barrier that was difficult to overcome.
18. Allon Schoener, ed., *Portal to America: The Lower East Side, 1870-1925* (New York: Holt, Rinehart and Winston, 1967), p. 11.
19. Issue of July 8, 1915, cited in *The American Jewish Year Book 5685 (1924-25),* pp. 350-351.
20. Hutchins Hapgood, *The Spirit of the Ghetto* (New York: Schocken Books, 1967), pp. 47-48.
21. Friedlaender, p. 369.
22. Herberg, p. 10.

23. Nathaniel Weyl, *The Jew in American Politics* (New Rochelle, New York: Arlington House, 1968), p. 78. It should be noted that while the percentage increase is slightly less than six-fold, because of the great increase in the total population of the United States, the actual increase represented is far more than six times the number of Jews who were in America in 1880.

24. Elbogen, pp. 225-226.

25. Quoted in: Dena Wilansky, *Sinai to Cincinnati: Lay Views on the Writings of Isaac M. Wise, Founder of Reform Judaism in America* (New York: Renaissance Book Co., 1937), pp. 178-179

26. A *landsmanschaft* was a mutual assistance society of families who came originally from the same town or area of the Pale of Settlement.

27. Peter Wiernik, *History of the Jews in America* (New York: The Jewish History Publishing Co., 1931), p. 266.

28. For a fuller biography see: *The Jewish Encyclopedia* Vol. VI (New York & London: Funk & Wagnalls Co., 1904), p. 325.

29. See: Solomon Grayzel, *A History of the Contemporary Jews* (New York: Meridan Books, Inc., and Philadelphia: The Jewish Publication Society of American, 1960), pp. 49-50; Sachar, p. 316; and Wiernik, pp. 266-270.

30. Harold U. Faulkner, *Politics, Reform and Expansion* (New York: York: Harper Torchbooks of Harper and Row, Publishers, 1959), p. 2.

31. Nathan Glazer, *American Judaism* (Chicago: University of Chicago Press, 1957), p. 80

32. Herberg, p. 178

33. Sachar, p. 318.

34. David A. Shannon, *The Socialist Party of America* (Chicago: Quadrangle Books, 1967), p. 8.

35. Rosten, pp. IX-XXV.

36. Rischin, p. 117

37. Abraham Cahan, "The Russian Jew in the United States," in *The Russian Jew in the United States*, Charles S. Bernheimer, ed. (Philadelphia: The John C. Winston Co., 1905), pp. 34-35

38. For an extensive listing of periodicals see: Rischin, pp. 115-123

39. Golden in Hapgood, p. 186.

40. Rischin, pp. 126-127; see also Milton Hindus, *The Old East Side* (Philadelphia; the Jewish Publication Society of America, 1969), p. SVII.

41. Shannon, pp. 185-186, 245.

42. Golden in Hapgood, p. 188

43. Hapgood, p. 138.

44. Cited in George M. Prince, "The Russian Jews in America," *Publication of the American Jewish Historical Society*, Vol. XLVII, No. 2 (December 1958)p. 133.

45. There were two kinds of elementary schools: the *heder* and the *Talmud Torah.* The *heder* (which means "room," and probably refers to the schoolroom in which the teacher both lived and taught) was a private school, usually run by the one teacher for a small number of students. The *Talmud Torah* was community sponsored, usually with several teachers and a number of classes. The *yeshiva* (which means "session") was an advanced academy for the detailed study of traditional literature, especially the Talmud. This was not necessarily for rabbinical training, but was designed rather to train all men in the wisdom of the tradition. For more detailed information see: Mark Zborowski and Elizabeth Herzog, *Life Is With People* (New York: Schocken Books, 1952), pp. 88-123; Simon Greenberg, "Jewish Educational Institutions," in *The Jews; Their History, Culture and Religion,* Louis Finkelstein, ed., 3rd edition (Philadelphia: The Jewish Publication Society of America, 1960), Vol. II, pp. 1254-1287.

46. Friedlaender, p. 370.

47. Menahem M. Edelstein, "History of the Development of a Jewish Teaching Profession in America," *Jewish Education* XXIII, No. 1 (Winter, 1952), p. 38

48. Earlier offers by the Russian government to provide education for Jewish children had usually proved to be veiled attempts to liquidate Jewish culture. For example: the state schools opened by Nicholas I in 1840 offered a full range of secular as well as religious studies. In order to encourage the acceptance of these

schools by Jews, the Czar hired Max Lilienthal, a German trained rabbi, to head the school system. It soon became apparent to Lilienthal, as has been suspected by the Russian Jews, that Jewish studies would be subordinate in these schools and that their sole purpose was Russification. As soon as he discovered the duplicity of the Czar's plan, Lilienthal emigrated from Russia to the United States. For a more detailed account of this see: S. M. Dubnow, *History of the Jews in Russia and Poland,* trans. I Friedlaender, (Philadelphia: The Jewish Publication Society of America, 1918). Vol. II, pp. 52-59, 136-137.

49. Among the congregations attempting to form day schools were Congregation B'nai Jeshurun, Cincinnati, 1840; Congregation Rodeph Shalom, Philadelphia, 1841; Temple Emanu-El, New York, 1845; Kehilath Anshe Maariv, Chicago, 1853; and the Sinai Congregation of Chicago, 1861. It is interesting to note that all of these congregations later affiliated with the Reform Movement.

50. Menahem M. Edelstein, "History of the Development of a Jewish Teaching Profession in America," in *Jewish Education,* XXIII, No. 2 (Summer, 1953), pp. 48-50. Note that the pay for teachers was about half that of factory workers.

51. See Solomon Grayzel, *A History of the Jews* (Philadelphia: The Jewish Publication Society of America, 1947), p. 691.

52. Alexander M. Dushkin, "Antaeus – Autobiographical Reflections," in *American Jewish Archives,* XXI, No. 2 (November, 1969), pp. 115-116.

53. Hutchins Hapgood, *The Spirit of the Ghetto* (New York: Funk and Wagnalls, 1909), pp. 44-45.

54. H. G. Good, *A History of American Education* (New York: The Macmillan Co., 1964), p. 140.

55. Edmund J. James, *The Immigrant Jew in America* (New York: B. F. Buck and Co., 1907), pp. 32-40, 184-199. Not all immigrant groups viewed with favor the opportunities provided by the American Public school system. Southern Italians, for example, viewed the public schools with a great deal of hostility. See: Herbert J. Gans, *The Urban Villagers* (New York: The Free Press, 1965), p. 205.

56. Dr. Samson Benderly, "Aims and Activities of the Bureau of Education of the Jewish Community (Kehillah) of New York, 1912," In *Jewish Education,* XX, No. 3 (Summer, 1949), pp. 92-109. This article was originally published as a pamphlet, "Publication No. 5," in 1912.

57. Will Herberg, "Religion and Education in America," *Religious Perspectives in American Life,* James Ward Smith and A. Leland Jamison, ed. (Princeton, N.J.: Princeton University Press, 1961), pp. 24-25.

58. Survey cited in: Weyl, p. 79.

59. Friedlaender, p. 374.

60. See Emanuel Gamoran, "Jewish Education in the United States, *"Studies in Religious Education,* Philip Lotz and L. W. Crawford, ed, (Nashville: Cokesbury Press, 1931), pp. 501-503.

61. Edelstein, p. 45

62. Leo L. Honor, "Jewish Education in the United States," in *The Jewish People, Past and Present,* Vol. II (New York: Jewish Encylclopedia Handbooks, Inc., 1948), p. 156.

63. Menahem M. Edelstein, "History of the Development of a Jewish Teaching Profession in America," in *Jewish Education,* XXIII, No. 3 (Fall, 1952), p. 35. For a more complete account of the new schools which were established during this period see. Leo L. Honor, "Jewish Elementary Education in the United States (1901-1950), "in *Publication of the American Jewish Historical Society,* XLIII, No. 1 (September, 1952), pp. 10-16.

64. The *kehillah* was an all-encompassing Jewish community organization which regulated all aspects of Jewish life. The New York Kehillah was an attempt to reconstruct the social setting of the small Russian and Polish Jewish villages, under the domination of wealthy and Americanized "German" leaders.

65. Alexander M. Dushkin, *Jewish Education in New York City* (New York: Bureau of Jewish Education, 1918), pp. 110-128.

66. This was not the case with all immigrant groups. The Report of the United States Immigration Commission I (1911) noted: "Among the immigration as a whole the tendency to become naturalized citizens, even among those who have been here five years or more is not great, although much more pronounced in some races

71

than others." Cited in: Edith Abbot, *Immigration: Select Documents and Case Records* (Chicago: University of Chicago Press, 1924), p. 548.

67. Isaac B. Berkson, *Theories of Americanization* (New York: Teachers College of Columbia University, 1920), p. 178.

68. Rischin, p. 101.

69. Ezekiel Lifschutz, "Yiddish Autobiographies as a Source of American Jewish History," *Publication of the American Jewish Historical Society,* Vol. LIII, No. 3 (March 1964) (New York: The American Jewish Historical Society, 1964), p. 253.

70. An estimated 87,000 East Europeans arrived in the years 1820-1880. For the first time this created a discernable East European Jewish group, others having come individually or by single families and blended into the existing community. See: Lifschutz, p. 253.

71. For more detailed information see: Wiernik, pp. 189-192; also reference in Hyman B. Grinstein, *The Rise of the Jewish Community in New York, 1965-1860* (Philadelphia: The Jewish Publication Society of America, 1947).

72. Oscar Handlin, *Adventure in Freedom* (New York: McGraw Hill Book Co., Inc., 1954), p. 114.

THE AMERICAN PERIOD

The End of Immigration:

Pressure to end, or at least, severely limit immigration had been building off and on for some fifty years before the restrictive laws of the 1920's curtailed immigration. On the West Coast, fear of economic competition led to the Chinese Exclusion Act of 1882. Due in large part to pressure by the Knights of Labor, which represented some 700,000 American workers, the importation of contract labor was prohibited by federal law in 1885. Also in the 1880's a head tax was levied on all immigrants; by 1907 this tax had been raised to four dollars per immigrant. The Agrarian, Nativist and Progressive movements of the late 19th and early 20th centuries, supported by such organizations as the American Protective League, The American Super-Race Foundation, the Asiatic Exclusion League, The Populists and the Ku Klux Klan advocated the ending of immigration. These groups felt that with the influx of a great number of foreigners, the "essential Americanism" of the country would dissappear and that "American" traditions and ideals would be submerged into inferior "foreign" ones.

Initially the restrictionists had little success. The period between 1900 and 1917 was basically one of economic prosperity in the United States, and during the first decade of the twentieth century 8,790,000 immigrants were admitted to the United States.[1] In 1897, 1911 and 1915 the United States Congress approved laws requiring that immigrants pass a literacy test. However, each of these bills was vetoed (by Presidents Cleveland, Taft and Wilson) and none became law. After World War I the restrictionists received added support and were able to enact a literacy test bill over President Woodrow Wilson's veto.

There were a number of reasons for this change in policy. Americans had become generally suspicious of aliens. The advent of peace brought a slowing of the economy. The new pseudo-scientific doctrine of Eugenics (put forth by a number of advocates, including Harry Loughlin, the government's Eugenics Agent) convinced many, especially the "100% American" groups like the D.A.R., the American Legion, and other "patriotic" groups, that the "genetically inferior" southern and eastern Europeans would "mongrelize" the "pure American blood lines." Also the labor unions, which were both vocal and influential by this time, maintained organized labor's traditional opposition to the importation of cheap immigrant labor.

In 1921 the restrictionists won their first major victory. In February of that year Congress passed a comprehensive immigration bill fixing quotas for each European country, but this was vetoed by President Wilson. Immediately after his inauguration, President Warren G. Harding called a special session of Congress for the purpose of re-submitting the same legislation, which he then signed. This bill set each nation's quotas at 3% of the number of Americans who had come from that country according to the 1910 census. The law was originally effective for one year, but it was renewed annually until 1924.

The most severe restriction on immigration was approved by Congress in 1924. Directed especially against southern and eastern Europeans, the Johnson-Reed Immigration Act set the quotas at 2% of the number from each country who were living in the United States as of the 1890 census *(i.e.,* before the years of great immigration from southern and eastern Europe.).

In the wake of the depression, President Herbert Hoover announced that he was determined to stop all immigration. He feared that under the conditions then prevailing, all immigrants were likely to become public wards. This further restricted the dwindling number of Jewish immigrants who were able to enter the United States.[2]

Immigration Statistics

From 1925 to 1939, approximately 2,500,000 immigrants came to the United States, compared to the period of 1900 to 1914 when 13,300,000 immigrants entered the country. Between 1920 and 1929, immigration amounted to a little more than 4,000,000, or less than half the number of immigrants between 1900 and 1909; from 1930 to 1939 about 700,000 immigrants entered the country, the lowest since a century before when, in the decade 1830 through 1839, immigration amounted to 538,000. The full effects of the 1924 act were not felt until after 1929.[3] Jewish immigration, which rose rapidly after World War I, was similarly curtailed. Over 119,000 had immigrated in 1921 (many were hurried in to beat the first restrictive laws), and about 50,000 came in each of the next three years. From 1925 to 1930, total Jewish immigration was between 10,000 and 12,500 per year; and from 1931 to 1933 it declined from 5,692 to 2,372.[4]

In 1933 Adolph Hitler became chancellor of Germany. With his ascent to power, the most violent form of anti-Semitism known to man took place. Many Jewish refugees from Germany sought sanctuary in the United States. However, the restrictive quota law of 1924 severely limited the United States as a refuge from the persecution of the Nazis and the oppressive governments in Roumania, Poland and Hungary. American refugee policy during the Nazi era did little to help Jewish refugees who wanted to enter the United States. State Department personnel, with a few exceptions, created an elaborate system of bureaucratic red tape which hindered, rather than helped, those seeking refuge from the Nazi terror.[5] Between the years 1933 and 1945 only about

170,000 Jews entered the United States; and the refugee program after 1947 added approximately 100,000.[6] Although these numbers were relatively small, included in this group were some 1,500 scholars and teachers, including Nobel Prize winners Albert Einstein and James Franck.[7] After 1948 most Jews who emigrated from Europe, North Africa and the Near East went to the newly formed State of Israel. Because of restrictive immigration laws in the United States and the unlimited immigration policies of Israel, this pattern still continues.

Anti-Semitism

In the United States, the government-organized and government-abetted Judeophobia which was so common in Europe (in contrast to an individual's personal anti-Jewish feeling) has never, for all intents and purposes, occurred. Legalized religious discrimination has generally been considered un-American, and religious freedom one of America's first principles. Despite this, overt anti-Semitism has arisen from time to time, reflecting the attitude of special interest groups or as a reaction to times of crisis.

As the number of Jewish immigrants coming from Europe diminished, anti-Jewish activities were increasingly aimed at the American Jewish community or at Jews-in-general. The 1920's and 1930's witnessed the rise of organized anti-Semitism in the United States. The Ku Klux Klan preached "100-per-cent-Americanism" and was heavily anti-Semitic. The revived Klan grew to between four and five million members, and spread throughout the United States.

The Protocols of the Elders of Zion, a little book probably based on the French *Dialogues in Hell* (ca. 1870) and devised by the Czar's secret police, was spread throughout the United States.[8] "It purported to record the proceedings, in Prague, of a secret body, plotting by means of the gold standard to capture the world on behalf of international Jewry. This flimsy story, so clearly fraudulent on the face of it, passed through edition after edition, and found credence among thousands of well-intentioned, if uncritical Americans who lived in a world in which truth was not separate from fiction and in which the idealistic promises of the war had led to betrayal."[9] The *Protocols* found an American champion in the person of Henry Ford and his *Dearborn Independent.* Ford's thesis was that the Jewish Question had been around for a long time, that the International Jew controlled every aspect of power, and, therefore, nothing remained for the Christian.[10] In 1927, as a result of much pressure and a series of libel suits, Ford issued a public apology to Louis Marshall, President of the American Jewish Committee, for his attack on Jews, but the damage caused by his anti-Semitic campaigns could not be easily repaired.[11] In addition, the rallies, radio broadcasts and publications of preachers such as Gerald L. K. Smith and Father Charles Coughlin were instrumental in spreading anti-Semitism in America.[12]

The following statement by an anonymous writer in 1928 shows some of the difficulties which the American Jews underwent at that time.

> The task is no easy one. Antagonisms become audible; social antipathies, group hostilities will not be silenced. To the more vivid newcomers, the background seems not only stern but bleak, colorless in its repressions and restraints. On Anglo-Saxon ears the new and quicker rhythm of alien peoples jangles bizarre, undisciplined, dangerous. Tolerance is urged, and even practiced on both sides. But conscious tolerance is the surest sign of deep and subtle misunderstanding.
>
> The Jew is a case in point. He is the most assimilated and assimilating being on the American scene - - and still an alien being. Passionately, at times pathetically, anxious to "belong" - - his clothes, his books, his beard, his diet, his mind have been refashioned to suit American conditions and conventions. He will not, he wills not to be different. [13]

During periods of economic depression, hostility towards Jews has increased. In America, this hostility was encouraged during the 1930's by the fact that a few Jews (along with a few Christians, it must be added) made money during this period while other Americans (including most Jews) were experiencing severe economic deprivation. In addition, Jewish support for the "revolutionary" New Deal again brought forth the cliches about "alien revolutionaries." Organized anti-Jewish hostility made its greatest gains in the United States during the Great Depression era of the 1930's, when nativist, anti-alien and protectionist fellings ran high. These feelings, combined with the racist theories propounded by the Nazis in Germany, provided a convenient rationale for those who wished to view Jews as their greatest enemy and the source of all their troubles.

Among the common techniques of the modern anti-Semite was the contention, self evidently contradictory but expressed with great conviction, that Jews simultaneously: (a) controlled world finance and were preparing to dominate the world by means of their supposed control of the sources of established power; and (b) Jews were, as a class, arch-revolutionaries intent on controlling the world by destroying financial and governmental institutions and bringing about total anarchy. It is evident that no rational defense can be made against accusations of this sort. It is equally evident that such a charge incorporates the fear that every favored institution is immediately endangered by some all-pervasive, omnipotent, incomprehensible force. This charge has had great emotional (albeit irrational) appeal to people in crisis. Though Jews have borne their full share of deprivation in times of depression and unemployment, many suffering American Christians believed that the Jew caused everyone's misfortune.

A "Red Scare" started in the early 1920's continued and grew into the 1930's. Jews, who were often pictured as being among the foremost "alien revolutionaries," were favored targets for witch-hunters. To combat this situation *The Christian Century* reported the results of a survey of the American Communist Party. "According to this investigation less than three percent of American communists are Jews. Moreover this survey shows that out of the two million Jews in this city [New York] there are only two thousand enrolled in the communist party. Also it is pointed out that the outstanding leaders of the movement here, such as Earl Browder, Clarence Hathaway and William Z. Foster, are all non-Jewish.[14]

During the 1930's, 121 American organizations included anti-Semitism as part of their *raison d'etre.* Some were openly pro-Nazi (such as the German-American Bund and the Silver Shirts); others used the guise of patriotic Americanism (for example, The Order of '76 and the Paul Reveres); and others advocated their own version of Christian supremacy (for example, Defenders of the Christian Faith and the American Christian Defenders).[15]

Social anti-Semitism - - Jews being refused admission to "restricted" country clubs, resorts, and residential areas - - was not unusual in the 1920's, 1930's and 1940's. In addition, many colleges and professional schools set up "quota" systems by which only a small percentage of Jews would be admitted, no matter their qualifications.

> In the 1930's medical schools set tight quotas limiting the entry of Jewish students. These practices were often kept secret, but we know a good deal of them. For example, the Cornell University Medical School, located in New York City, limited Jewish students to their proportion in the state of New York, that is, to about 1 in 7. Thus, of 80 places the Cornell school had in 1940, 10 were to be for Jews, 70 for non-Jews. But 7 of every 12 applicants were Jews. Thus 1 of 70 Jewish applicants and 1 of 7 non-Jewish applicants were admitted. So boys seeking entry to medical school took as a fact of life that bright Jews would be rejected in favor of much less bright non-Jews - - and this even when both were undergraduates at Cornell and knew perfectly well how one another stood in class.[16]

Jews also knew that they could not expect to get certain jobs; for example, there were few Jewish engineers or college professors until the late 1940's.

Since the 1940's overt anti-Semitism has declined dramatically. While many barriers have fallen, even today it is extremely difficult for a Jew to rise to the upper executive positions in such fields as banking, insurance, college administration and the giant industrial corporations. However, except for residual "polite" anti-Jewishness and occasional outbursts related to the Civil Rights Movement or the State of Israel, anti-Semitism is not a main factor in American life.

Cultural Pluralism

One of the ongoing conflicts in American life has involved the definition of "Americanization." Basically the major points of view may be summarized in the phrases "melting pot" and "cultural pluralism." Those who supported the "melting pot" concept believed that America is a great crucible in which all immigrant groups are homogenized into a uniform "American" type. Those who supported "cultural pluralism" believed that America did not require immigrants to forsake their particular cultural heritage, but rather encouraged each group to maintain its own identity while also becoming part of America.

Among the foremost popularizers of the "melting-pot" concept was the influential educational philosopher John Dewey. Dewey contended that immigrants should be divested of their ethnic character and be indoctrinated in the ways of those who embodied "the real America."[17] After World War I there was a fiece drive to make America a melting-pot. This was dramtically illustrated when the state of Oregon passed a law requiring all children between the ages of eight and sixteen to attend the public schools. This kind of compulsory public school education law was declared unconstitutional by the United States Supreme Court in 1925.[18]

Although the melting-pot provided a convenient image, cultural pluralism better describes the reality of American life. "What is incontrovertible and significant, in any case, is the 'fact' of religious pluralism. There is no indication that the pattern will be altered in any foreseeable future."[19] Cultural Pluralism may have begun as "the transplanting of European multinational multicultural society to America,"[20] but it soon became an accepted American point of view. By the 1920's such social scientists as Robert E. Park, Franz Boas and E. Franklin Frazier were spokesmen for cultural pluralism. They contended that American democracy would be enriched by allowing ethnic groups to maintain their separate characteristics, rather than encouraging them to melt into a uniform American culture.[21]

The concept of cultural pluralism was widely accepted by Jewish social scientists and educators. Horace Kallen repudiated the idea of melting-pot Americanism. He rejected assimilationism and pictured instead an America that would be "a federation or commonwealth of nationalities."[22]   Israel Friedlaender, Mordecai M. Kaplan, Emanuel Gamoran and others adopted this point of view and made it one of the underlying premises of all their work.

Like other immigrant groups who wanted to become part of the American scene, the Jewish community was faced with the problem of determining how far one may go before he is too Americanized and, therefore, surrenders his traditional culture. Leaders of the Jewish community wanted the Jew to be able to function and survive in the United States, but not become so much assimilated that they would lose their traditional Jewish heritage. "Now that so many of these barriers are down, the Jews have become less Jewish and more prosperous, there are tendencies to caution and withdrawal. A satisfying pattern of Jewish middle-class life has not yet emerged. This failure in Jewish life reflects the general unease of American middle-class life, as well as the specific Jewish dilemma of finding, in this amorphous society, a balance between separation and the loss of identity." [23]

This dilemma, which has faced and is facing all ethnic minority groups, does not lend itself to easy solution. Every group and every individual continually finds and redefines its place in American culture.

The Home-Born

Fifty years ago almost the entire American Jewish community either had been born in Europe, or had a parent or several grandparents born in Europe. Although a large percentage were American born, the Jewish religious culture of the 1920's was still essentially that which had been imported from Eastern Europe.

The children and grandchildren of these immigrants are today culturally and emotionally American, and the vast majority of them have remained Jewish. A national group consciousness has grown among American Jews, created and nurtured by a variety of influences. Because of European memories, life in Depression Era America and the reaction to the Hitlerian holocaust, there is an ever-present uneasiness that anti-Semitism will recur and a realization that the future security of the Jewish community may depend on forces and events beyond its control. The creation of the State of Israel gave an added dimension to the religious interests of most American Jews. The federation movement in Jewish philanthropy; the activities of almost 300 national Jewish organizations, whose interests include all aspects of culture, domestic and overseas philanthropy, and community relations; and the formation of such umbrella organizations as the National Council of Jewish Federations and Welfare Funds, the National Community Relations Advisory Committee and the Conference of Presidents have created a degree of emotional and eleemosynary unity. In addition, an important influence has been the American religious environment, which groups religion into three great categories: Protestant, Catholic and Jew, each of which is an umbrella term; and the American expectation that people will belong to a religious community and be a member of "a church."

The Americianizing trend of the American Jewish community is evidenced by the development of the Jewish press in the United States. The German language periodicals, which numbered eleven in 1900, had declined to one in 1915 and completely disappeared by 1925. Yiddish language publications, which numbered eighty-two in 1900 (including several dailies) fell to forty-one by 1915, to thirty by 1925 and to twenty-two (including occasional publications and children's magazines) by the 1960's. Jewish periodicals in English numbered sixty-nine at the turn of the century (this count also included a number of congregational newsletters), rose to ninety-one by 1915, and currently numbers more than 160, (counting only regularly published newspapers, journals and magazines).[24]

Jews in America have maintained an active participation in the entertainment media and in all the fine arts. Since World War II both Jewish and non-Jewish writers have made increasing use of Jews as fictional characters in popular novels and plays. During the 1960's many of the "best-seller" novels were by Jewish authors writing about Jews. Commercial television has given the Americanized Jew nationwide visibility as actor, performing artist, entertainer, news reporter, sportscaster, athlete and news maker; and many popular series have included stories about Jews. Jews have remained among the most enthusiastic supporters of American cultural endeavors, both traditional and modernist. "There is little doubt that America's Jews have been in the vanguard . . . in some instances as culture initiators, in other as culture bearers, and everywhere as culture consumers."[25]

In reaction to the rise of Hitler and because of the already pro-Zionist sympathies of the East European Jews, American Jewry took on a pro-Zionist view. Many American Jews contributed to the establishment of the State of Israel, and Jews in the United States generally rejoiced in the establishment of a Jewish state. However, the *aliyah* (emigration to Israel) movement made little progress. American Jews were too well assimilated, accepted and happy in the United States. "As for Zionism as an ideology, that escape vanished with the establishment of Israel. The few who imagined they would themselves migrate to the promised land and the larger number who expected that from it would emanate the influences to redeem the life of the Jews in exile were alike disappointed. When the long-awaited day finally came, there was no exodus. In vain persuasive voices urged the confirmed Zionists to migrate. They would not go. With the way open, they discovered at once that it was not on that far Mediterranean shore they belonged, but where they were in America."[26] Since 1948, Zionism in America has meant only sympathy for Israel, study about Israel and financial contributions to the United Jewish Appeal and the other agencies which raise funds for immigrant settlement and for medical, social or education programs in Israel.

By the 1930's the Reform movement had become more moderate in its approach to Judaism and the Jewish people. Reform leaders began to see new values in old ceremonials and in the Hebrew language. Members of proud old families slowly softened their attitude toward the newly-Americanized East European Jews, who were now becoming part of the Reform movement (and, by marriage, part of their families) in increasing numbers. The rise of Hitlerism in Germany and overt manifestations of anti-Semitism in America stimulated sympathy for Zionism and awakened Reform Jews to the reality that all Jews, regardless of origin or ritual preferences, shared the same fate in times of trouble. Reform discarded the ideas that distinctive religious customs had to be eliminated and that support of Zionism might somehow compromise their loyalty as Americans. This change was shown not only in the reintroduction of many traditional customs and rituals[27] and the support given to such groups as the Zionist Organization of America and the United Jewish Appeal, but especially through the educational system of the Reform movement.

Emanuel Gamoran, the Director of Education of the Union of American Hebrew Congregations from 1923 to 1958, took the position that the immigrant must adjust to America, but in turn he must not be required to give up his individuality. Demanding that the immigrant be "an American type" is asking him to be something that does not exist, and it very often destroys old values which would be a good contribution to America. The Sunday School and adult study materials published while he was educational director reflected the view that loyalty to the United States could not be developed through disloyalty to one's ethnic group. Like Kallen, he believed that America does not desire uniformity, but rather a like-mindedness, and that true democracy encourages the preservation of distinctive group values. He believed that to be truly American, every group should develop itself culturally and, therefore, contribute its best qualities to American life.[28]

These new attitudes also found expression in a revised statement of principles for the Reform movement. In 1937 the Central Conference of American Rabbis, at their meeting in Columbus, Ohio, issued a new statement, the "Guiding Principles of Reform Judaism." It was intended "not as a fixed creed but as a guide for the progressive elements of Jewry."

The first part of the platform reiterated the idea of progressive revelation and the harmony of Judaism with scientific knowledge. It then introduced several principles which were quite different from the "Pittsburgh Platform" of 1885. The Torah, both "written" and "oral" (i.e. both the Bible and the rabbinic tradition), is the moral law on which each age builds for its own time. All Jews share a group loyalty due to a common history and faith. Jews are loyal citizens of the country in which they reside, but are also obligated to help in the rebuilding of Palestine. Israel has the Mission to work in cooperation with all mankind to bring about the Messianic Age.

The second part of the platform stated that religion and morality blend into an indissoluble unity. Judaism affirms the sanctity and worth of human life and personality, and seeks justice for all and the attainment of a just society.

The third part stated that Jews should participate in all aspects of Jewish communal life and that the home must continue to be the stronghold of Judaism, promoting morality and religious devotion. The synagogue is the primary communal agency by which Judaism is fostered and preserved; it links the Jews of each community and unites them with all Israel.[29] Judaism as a way of life requires preservation of the Sabbath and Holy Days, the keeping and developing of inspirational ceremonies, the cultivation of religious art and music, and the use of Hebrew with the vernacular in worship and education.[30]

In the 1930's a new movement known as Reconstructionism began. Reflecting the views of cultural pluralism held by its founder, Dr. Mordecai M. Kaplan, it sought to reconstruct the various segments of American Jewry into an "organic community." Kaplan's main thesis is that Judaism is a civilization, with the Jewish religion as expressed in the synagogue, school and community center, as its chief expression.[31] In Reconstructionism, nationalism is interpreted in terms of being a cultural concept which includes land, language, literature, religion, laws and social organization.[32]

In summarizing Kaplan's views one must comprehend that he sees Judaism surviving only if it meets the real needs of men. He sees Judaism as an evolving religious civilization which adjusts itself to the conditions within which it exists. Judaism is an ongoing civilization or culture which must retain its cultural identity; have a homeland in Palestine; renew the historic covenant with Jews all over the world binding them into one 'Peoplehood'; develop organic Jewish communities with the aim of furthering Jewish religion, peoplehood, and culture; and revitalize the Jewish religion through the study of it in the spirit of free inquiry and maintaining the separation of church and state. The belief in God is interpreted in universal as well as Jewish experience. Jews must learn to live in two civilizations - - its historic one and the one of its present environment; and the Jewish people must maintain the traditional concept of the Torah, since it is considered to be such an integral part of Jewish civilization covering the ethical, spiritual and cultural experiences of the Jews. Kaplan also insists that for the Jews to maintain their cultural identity, they must emphasize the heroes, festivals, magnificent events, places and traditions of the total Jewish experience.

Although Reconstructionism has not built a large nationally organized movement as other branches of Judaism did, Reconstructionist philosophy has had a great influence on the American Jewish community through its adoption by many members of the Reform and Conservative movements.

★ ★ ★

In a little over 300 years a distinguishable and distinguished American Jewish community has developed. The community is religio-culturally Jewish; but in appearance, language, dress, interests, occupations, attitudes, values and names it is typically American. The United States has been good to the Jew. It has given him virtually unlimited freedom and opportunity. In turn, the Jew has displayed an intense desire to become part of America, to succeed and contribute to the making of America. The Jew has taken full advantage of the opportunities which America has offered him, and his outstanding achievements in America have come in large measure because he has been *the eager immigrant*.

FOOTNOTES

For The American Period:

1. *Statistical Abstract of the United States, 1920* (Washington: Government Printing Office, 1921), pp. 100-101.

2. For a more complete study of immigration restrictions see: John Higham, *Strangers in the Land* (New York: Atheneum, 1963); See also relevant chapters in: Maldwyn Allen Jones, *American Immigration* (Chicago: University of Chicago Press, 1960) and Oscar Handlin, *The Uprooted* (New York: Grosset & Dunlop, 1951).

3. E.P. Hutchinson, "The New Immigration, *"The Annals of the American Academy of Political and Social Science,* CCCLXVII (September, 1966), p. 65.

4. American Jewish Year Book 5678 (1926-1927), p. 416; *The Universal Jewish Encyclopedia* (New York: The Universal Jewish Encyclopedia, Inc., 1942), Vol. VII, p. 550.

5. See: David S. Wyman, *Paper Walls: America and the Refugee Crisis* (Amherst: University of Massachusetts Press, 1968).

6. Oscar Handlin, *Adventures in Freedom* (New York: McGraw-Hill Book Company, 1954), p. 251.

7. Albert H. Friedlander, "Cultural Contributions of the German Jew in America, *"Jew from Germany in the United States,* Eric E. Hirshler, ed. (New York: Farrer, Straus and Cudahy, 1955), pp. 162-168.

8. For the texts and an extended discussion see: Herman Bernstein, *The Truth About "The Protocols of Zion"* (New York: Covici-Friede Publishers, 1935.)

9. Handlin, p. 203.

10. William C. Richards, *The Last Billionaire:* Henry Ford (New York: Bantam Books, Inc., 1956), p. 67.

11. See related correspondence in: Charles Reznikoff, ed., *Louis Marshall: Champion of Liberty,* 2 vols. (Philadelphia: The Jewish Publication Society of America, 1957).

12. For an excellent short study of anti-Semitism in America see: John Higham, "American Anti-Semitism Historically Reconsidered," Charles Herbert Stember and Others, *Jews in the Mind of America* (New York: Basic Books, Inc., 1966), pp. 237-258.

13. Analyticus, *Jews Are Like That* (New York: Brentano's, Inc., 1928) p. ix.

14. *The Christian Century,* September 5, 1934.

15. For a detailed study see: Donald S. Strong, *Organized Anti-Semitism in America: The Rise of Group Prejudice During the Decade 1930-40.* (Washington, D.C.: American Council on Public Affairs, 1941).

16. Nathan Glazer and Daniel Patrick Moynihan, *Beyond the Melting Pot* (Cambridge: M.I.T. Press, 1963), p. 156

17. See: John Dewey, *Democracy and Education* (New York: The Macmillan Company, 1916), pp. 94-116; See also: Lawrence Cremin, *The Transformation of the School* (New York: Vintage Press, 1961), p. 68. A popular play which gave the view that American was God's crucible, the great melting-pot where all the European races were melted and reformed was: Israel Zangwill, *The Melting Pot* (New York: The Macmillan Company, 1909).

18. A good account of this incident can be found in David B. Tyack, "The Perils of Pluralism: The Background of the Pierce Case," *The American Historical Review,* Vol LXXIV, No. 1 (October, 1968), pp. 74-98

19. A. Leland Jamison, "Religions on the Christian Perimeter," *The Shaping of American Religion,* eds. James Ward Smith and A. Leland Jamison (Princeton: Princeton University Press, 1961), pp. 162-163.

20. Will Herberg, *Protestant-Catholic-Jew* (Garden City: Doubleday & Company, Inc., (1960), p. 20.

21. Gilbert Osofsky, *Harlem: The Making of a Ghetto* (New York: Harper & Row, 1968), p. 182.

22. Eric F. Goldman, *Rendezvous with Destiny* (New York: RandomHouse Inc., 1956), p. 171. For a complete presentation of Kallen's views see: Horace M. Kallen, *Cultural Pluralism and the American Idea,* (Philadelphia: University of

Pennsylvania Press, 1956).

23. Glazer and Moynihan, p. 180.
24. *The American Jewish Year Book 5660 (1899-1900),* pp. 271-282; *5675 (1914-1915),* pp. 328-334; *5676 (1915-1916),* pp. 340-341; *5686 (1925-1926),* pp. 355-362; and *Volume 67 (1966),* pp. 523-530.
25. Morris N. Kertzer, *Today's American Jew* (New York: McGraw-Hill Book Company, 1967), p. 33.
26. Handlin, pp. 247-248.
27. See: Lawrence Siegel, "Reflections on Neo-Reform in the Central Conference of American Rabbis,: *American Jewish Archives,* Vol. XX, No. 1 (April, 1968) Cincinnati: The American Jewish Archives, 1968, pp. 63-83.
28. Emanuel Gamoran, *Changing Conceptions in Jewish Education* (New York: The Macmillan Company, 1924), II, pp. 44-46. For an intensive study of Emanuel Gamoran see: Robert J. Wechman, *Emanuel Gamoran,* Unpublished Ph. D. Dissertation, the Graduate School, Syracuse University, 1970.
29. "Israel" as used here is obviously intended to include the entirety of the Jewish community. This differs from the 19th century use of the word, in which "Israel" meant only "the enlightened segment."
30. *Yearbook: Central Conference of American Rabbis,* Vol. XLVII, 1937, pp. 97-100.
31. See: *The Jewish People: Past and Present* (New York: Jewish Encyclopedia Handbooks, 1955), IV, 137. See also: Mordecai M. Kaplan, "The Meaning of Reconstructionism," *The Reconstructionist,* Vol. VI, No. 1 (February 16, 1940).
32. See: Mordecai M. Kaplan, *Judaism As A Civilization* (New York: The MacMillan Company, 1935).

SELECTED BIBLIOGRAPHY
BOOKS

Abbot, Edith. *Immigration: Select Documents and Case Records.* Chicago: University of Chicago Press, 1924.

Abrahams, Israel. *Jewish Life in the Middle Ages.* London: Edward Goldston, Ltd., 1932.

Adler, Cyrus, and Aaron M. Margalith. *With Firmness in the Right.* New York: The American Jewish Committee, 1946.

Agar, Herbert. *The Saving Remnant: An Account of Jewish Survival.* New York: The Viking Press, 1960.

American Jewish Archives. 21 volumes.

American Jewish Yearbook. 70 volumes.

Analyticus, *Jews Are Like That!* New York: Brentano's Publishers, 1928.

Bamberger, Bernard J. ed. *Reform Judaism: Essays by Hebrew Union College Alumni.* Cincinnati: Hebrew Union College Press, 1949.

Baron, Salo W. *Modern Nationalism and Religion.* New York: Meridian Books, Inc., 1934.

Berkson, Isaac B. *Theories of Americanization.* New York: Teachers College, Columbia University, 1933.

Bernheimer, Charles S. *The Russian Jew in the United States.* Philadelphia: The John C. Winston Co., 1905.

Bernstein, Herman. *The Truth About "The Protocols of Zion".* New York: Covici-Friede Publishers, 1935.

Birmingham, Stephen. *Our Crowd.* New York: Dell Publishing Co., Inc., 1967.

Blau, Joseph L., and Baron, Salo W., ed. *The Jews of the United States, 1790-1840; A Documentary History.* Three Volumes. New York: Columbia University Press, and Philadelphia: The Jewish Publication Society of America, 1963.

Bogen, Boris D. *Jewish Philanthropy.* New York: The Macmillan Company, 1917.

Brinton, Crane. *Ideas and Men.* New York: Prentice-Hall, Inc., 1960.
          . *The Shaping of the Modern Mind* New York: New American Library, 1953.

Butler, Pierce. *Judah P. Benjamin.* Philadelphia: George W. Jacobs and Co., 1906.

Cohen, Arthur. *The Natural and Supernatural Jew.* New York: McGraw-Hill Book Company, 1964.

Cohen, George. *The Jews in the Making of America.* Boston: The Stratford Co., Publishers, 1924.

Cremin, Lawrence. *The Transformation of the School.* New York: Vintage Books, 1961.

Cronbach, Abraham. *Reform Movements in Judaism.* New York: Bookman Associates, Inc., 1963.

Davis, Moshe. *The Emergence of Conservative Judaism.* Philadelphia: The Jewish Publication Society of America, 1963.

Dewey, John. *The School and Society.* Chicago: The Macmillan Company, 1916.
          . *Democracy and Education.* New York: The Macmillan Company, 1916.

Dimont, Max I. *Jews, God and History.* New York: New American Library, 1962.

Dubnow, S. M. History of the Jews in Russia and Poland, I. Translated by I. Friendlaender. Philadelphia: The Jewish Publication Society of America, 1916.

Dushkin, Alexander M. *Jewish Education in New York City.* New York: The Bureau of Jewish Education, 1918.

Eaton, Clement. *The Growth of Southern Civilization.* New York: Harper Torchbooks, 1963.

Elbogen, Ismar. *A Century of Jewish Life,* trans. Moses Hadas. Philadelphia: The Jewish Publication Society of America, 1944.

Essays in American Jewish History. Cincinnati: The American Jewish Archives, 1958.

Faulkner, Harold U. *Politics, Reform and Expansion.* New York: Harper Torchbooks, 1959.

Finkelstein, Louis, ed. *The Jews: Their History, Culture, and Religion.* Two Volumes. New York: Harper & Brothers Publishers, 1960.

Freehof, Solomon B. *Reform Jewish Practice.* 2 vols. Cincinnati: Hebrew Union College Press, 1944-52.

Freund, Miriam K. *Jewish Merchants in Colonial America.* New York: Behrman's Jewish Book House, 1939.

Friedlaender, Israel. *The Jews of Russia and Poland.* New York: G. P. Putnam's Sons, 1915.

Friedman, Lee M. *Early American Jews.* Cambridge, Mass.: Harvard University Press, 1934.

Gamoran, Emanuel. *Changing Conceptions in Jewish Education.* Two volumes. New York: The Macmillan Company, 1924.

Gans, Herbert J. *The Urban Villagers.* New York: The Free Press, 1965.

Gipson, Lawrence Henry. *The Coming of the Revolution.* New York: Harper Torchbooks, 1962.

Glatzer, Nahum N., ed. *A Jewish Reader.* New York: Schocken Books, 1961.

Glazer, Nathan. *American Judaism.* Chicago: University of Chicago Press, 1957.

Glazer, Nathan and Moynihan, Daniel Patrick. *Beyond the Melting Pot.* Cambridge: M.I.T. Press, 1963.

Golden, Harry. *Only in America.* New York: Permabooks, 1959.

. *For 2¢ Plain.* New York: Permabooks, 1960.

Goldman, Eric F. *Rendezvous with Destiny.* New York: Random House, Inc., 1956.

Good, H. G. *A History of American Education.* New York: The Macmillan Co., 1964.

Graetz, Heinrich. *History of the Jews,* V. Philadelphia: The Jewish Publication Society of America, 1956.

Grayzel, Solomon. *A History of the Jews.* Philadelphia: The Jewish Publication Society of America, 1956.

. *A History of the Contemporary Jews.* New York and Philadelphia: Meridian Books, Inc. and The Jewish Publication Society of America, 1960.

Green, Thomas F. *Education and Pluralism: Ideal and Reality.* Syracuse, Syracuse University Press, 1966.

Grinstein, Hyman B. *The Rise of the Jewish Community of New York, 1654-1860.* Philadelphia: The Jewish Publication Society, 1947.

Grusd, Edward E. *B'nai B'rith: The Story of a Covenant.* New York: Appleton-Century, 1966.

Handlin, Oscar and Mary F. *Danger in Discord.* New York: The Anti-Defamation League of B'nai B'rith, 1948.

Handlin, Oscar. *The Uprooted.* New York: Grosset & Dunlop, Publishers 1951.

. *Adventures in Freedom.* New York: McGraw-Hill Book Company, 1954.

. *Race and Nationality in American Life.* Garden City: Doubleday Anchor Books, 1957.

. *A Continuing Task: The American Jewish Joint Distribution Committee, 1914-1964.* New York: Random House, 1964.

Halasz, Nicholas. *Captain Dreyfus: The Story of A Mass Hysteria.* New York: Grove Press, 1955.

Hapgood, Hutchins. *The Spirit of the Ghetto.* New York: Funk & Wagnalls Company, 1909.

. *The Spirit of the Ghetto.* Notes by Harry Golden. New York: Schocken Books, 1967.

Hayes, Carlton J. H. *A Generation of Materialism.* New York: Harper & Brothers, Publishers, 1941.

Hays, Samuel P. *The Response to Industrialism: 1885-1914.* Chicago: The University of Chicago Press, 1957.

Heller, James G. *Isaac Mayer Wise: His Life, Work and Thought.* New York: The Union of American Hebrew Congregations, 1965.

Hershkowitz, Leo. *Wills of Early New York Jews (1704-1799).* New York: The American Jewish Historical Society, 1967.

Hertz, Richard C. *The Education of the Jewish Child.* New York: Union of American Hebrew Congregations, 1953.

Hertzberg, Arthur. *The Zionist Idea.* New York: Meridian Books, Inc., 1960.

Higham, John. *Strangers in the Land.* New York: Atheneum, 1963.

Hindus, Milton. *The Old East Side.* Philadelphia: The Jewish Publication Society of America, 1969.

Hirshler, Eric E., ed. *Jews From Germany in the United States.* New York: Farrar, Straus and Cudahy, 1955.

James, Edmund J. *The Immigrant Jew in America.* New York: B. F. Buck & Co., 1907.

The Jewish Encyclopedia, 12 vols. New York: Funk and Wagnalls, 1901.

The Jewish People: Past and Present, 4 vols, New York: Jewish Encyclopedia Handbooks, Inc., 1955.

Jones, Maldwyn Allen, *American Immigration.* Chicago: University of Chicago

Kallen, Horace M. *Cultural Pluralism and the American Idea.* Philadelphia: University of Pennsylvania Press, 1956.

Kaplan, Mordecai M. *Judaism as a Civilization.* New York: The Macmillan Co., 1935.

. *The Meaning of God in Modern Jewish Religion.* New York: Behrman House, Inc., 1937.

. *The Future of the American Jew.* New York: The Macmillan Co., 1948.

Kertzer, Morris N. *Today's American Jew.* New York: McGraw-Hill Book Company, 1967.

Kohler, Kaufmann. *Jewish Theology.* New York: The Macmillan Co., 1918.

Kohn, Hans. *Nationalism: Its Meaning and History.* Princeton: D. Van Nostrand Company, Inc., 1955.

. *American Nationalism.* New York: Collier Books, 1961.

Korn, Bertram W. *American Jewry and the Civil War.* Philadelphia: The Jewish Publication Society of America, 1957.

. *The American Reaction to the Mortara Case: 1858-1859.* Cincinnati: The American Jewish Archives, 1957.

. *Jews and Negro Slavery in the Old South.* Elkins Park Pa.: Congregation Keneseth Israel, 1961.

Landa, M. J. *The Jew In Drama.* London: P.S. King and Son, Ltd., 1926.

Learsi, Rufus. *The Jews in America: A History.* Cleveland and New York: The World Publishing Co., 1954.

Levenson, Sam. *Everything But Money.* New York: Simon & Schuster, 1966.

Levinger, Lee J. *A History of the Jews in the United States.* New York: Union of American Hebrew Congregations, 1931.

Liptzin, Sol. *Generation of Decision.* New York: Bloch Publishing Co., 1958.

Lotz, Philip H. and Crawford, L. W., eds. *Studies in Religious Education.* Nashville: Cokesbury Press, 1931.

Mann, Arthur. *Yankee Reformers in the Urban Age.* New York: Harper & Row, Publishers, 1966.

Marcus, Jacob Rader. *Early American Jewry,* 2 vols. Philadelphia: The Jewish Publication Society of America, 1951-55.

. *Memoirs of American Jews,* 3 vols. Philadelphia: The Jewish Publication Society of America, 1955.

. *The Rise and Destiny of the German Jew.* Cincinnati: Union of American Hebrew Congregations. 1934.

. *Studies in American Jewish History.* Cincinnati: Hebrew Union College Press, 1969.

May, Max B. *Isaac Mayer Wise.* New York: G. P. Putnam's Sons, 1916.

Osofsky, Gilbert. *Harlem: The Making of a Ghetto.* New York: Harper & Row, 1968.

Packard, Vance. *The Status Seekers.* New York: Pocket Books, Inc., 1961.

Philipson, David. *The Reform Movement In Judaism.* New York: Macmillan Co., 1931.

. *My Life as an American Jew.* Cincinnati: John G. Kidd & Son, Inc., 1941.

Pinson, Koppel S. ed. *Essays on Anti-Semitism.* New York: Conference on Jewish Relations, 1942.

. *Modern Germany,* 2nd edition. New York: The Macmillan Company, 1966.

Plaut, W. Gunther. *The Growth of Reform Judaism.* New York: World Union for Progressive Judaism, Ltd., 1965.

Postal, Bernard, Silver, Jesse, Silver, Roy. *Encyclopedia of Jews in Sports.* New York: Bloch Publishing Company, 1965.

Reform Judaism: Essays by Alumni of the Hebrew Union College. Cincinnati: Hebrew Union College Press, 1949.

Report of the Commissioner of Education for the Year Ended June 30, 1913, I. Washington: Government Printing Office, 1914.

Reznikoff, Charles, ed., *Louis Marshall: Champion of Liberty,* 2 vols. Philadelphia: The Jewish Publication Society of America, 1957.

Reznikoff, Charles and Engelman, Uriah Z. *The Jews of Charleston.* Philadelphia: The Jewish Publication Society of America, 1950.

Ribalow, Harold U. *The Jew in American Sports.* New York: Bloch Publishing Company, 1963.

Richards, William C. *The Last Billionaire: Henry Ford.* New York: Bantam Books, Inc., 1956.

Riis, Jacob A. *How the Other Half Lives.* New York: Hill and Wang, 1957.

Rischin, Moses. *The Promised City.* Cambridge Mass.: Harvard University Press, 1962.

Rosten, Leo. *The Joys of Yiddish.* New York: Pocket Books, 1970.

Sabine, George H. *A History of Political Theory.* New York: Holt, Rhinehart and Winston, Inc., 1961.

Sachar, Abram L. *Sufference is the Badge.* New York: Alfred A. Knopf, 1939.

Schappes, Morris U. *A Documentary History of the Jews of the United States, 1654-1875,* rev. ed. New York: The Citadel Press, 1952.

Schermerhorn, R. A., *These Our People.* Boston: D. C. Heath and Company, 1949.

Schoener, Allon, ed. *Portal to America: The Lower East Side, 1870-1925.* New York: Holt, Rinehart and Winston, 1967.

Schwartzman, Sylvan D. *Reform Judaism in the Making.* New York: Union of American Hebrew Congregations, 1962.

Schwarz, Leo W., ed. *Great Ages and Ideas of the Jewish People.* New York: Random House, 1956.

Shannon, David A. *The Socialist Party of America.* Chicago: Quadrangle Books, 1967.

Silberman, Lou H. *American Impact: Judaism in the United States in the Early Nineteenth Century.* Syracuse: Syracuse University Press, 1964.

Simonhoff, Harry. *Jewish Participants in the Civil War.* New York: ARCO Publishing Company, Inc., 1963.

Sklare, Marshall. *The Jews.* Glencoe, Illinois: The Free Press, 1958.

Smith, James Ward and Jamison, A. Leland, eds. *The Shaping of American Religion,* Princeton: Princeton University Press, 1961.

————. *Religious Perspectives in American Culture,* Princeton: Princeton University Press, 1961.

Stember, Charles Herbert and Others. *Jews in the Mind of America.* New York: Basic Books, Inc., 1966.

Statistical Abstract of the United States, 1920. Washington: Government Printing Office, 1921.

Strong, Donald S. *Organized Anti-Semitism in America: The Rise of Group Prejudice During the Decade 1930-40.* Washington, D.C.: American Council On Public Affairs, 1941.

Straus, Oscar S. *Origin of Republican Form of Government.* New York: G. P. Putnam's Sons, 1885.

Union Prayerbook for Jewish Worship: Newly Revised Edition. Cincinnati: Central Conference of American Rabbis, 1940.

Universal Jewish Encyclopedia, 10 vols. New York: The Universal Jewish Encyclopedia, 1939.

Wechman, Robert J. *Emanuel Gamoran.* Unpublished Ph. D. dissertation, The Graduate School, Syracuse University, 1970.

Weyl, Nathaniel. *The Jew in American Politics.* New Rochelle, N.Y.: Arlington House, 1968.

Wiernik, Peter. *History of the Jews in America.* New York: The Jewish History Publishing Co., 1912, rev. ed. 1931.

Wilansky, Dena. *Sinai to Cincinnati.* New York: Renaissance Book Co., 1937.

Wirth, Louis *The Ghetto.* Chicago: University of Chicago Press, 1928.

Wise, Isaac Mayer. *Reminiscences.* Cincinnati: Leo Wise and Co., 1901.

Wittke, Carl. *We Who Built America.* Cleveland: Case Western Reserve University Press, 1964.

Wolf, 2nd, Edwin and Whiteman, Maxwell. *The History of the Jews of Philadelphia from Colonial Times to the Age of Jackson.* Philadelphia: The Jewish Publication Society of America, 1957.

Wyman, David S. *Paper Walls: America and the Refugee Crisis.* Amherst: University of Massachusetts Press, 1968.

Yaffe, James. *The American Jews.* New York: Paperback Library, 1969.

Yearbook. Central Conference of American Rabbis, 79 vols.

Zborowski, Mark and Herzog, Elizabeth. *Life Is With People.* New York: Schocken Books, 1952.

Zielonka, David M. *Introduction to a Dictionary of American Jewish Biography, 1649-1962.* Unpublished Master of Arts Thesis, Hebrew Union College-Jewish Institute of Religion, Cincinnati, 1962.

ARTICLES

Benderly, Samson. "Aims and Activities of the Bureau of Education of the Jewish Community (Kehillah) of New York, 1912." *Jewish Education,* XX (Summer, 1949), 92-109.

The Christian Century, September 5, 1934.

Dushkin, Alexander M. "What is American Jewish Education." *Education* (May, 1933), 540-45.

———. "Antaeus-Autobiographical Reflections." *American Jewish Archives,* XXI, No. 2 (November, 1969), 113-39.

Edelstein, Menachem M. "History of the Development of a Jewish Teaching Profession in America." *Jewish Education,* XXIII, No. 1 (Winter, 1952), 36-42, 62.

———. "History of the Development of a Jewish Teaching Profession in America." *Jewish Education,* XXIII, No. 2 (Summer, 1952), 45-53, 68.

———. "History of the Development of a Jewish Teaching Profession in America." *Jewish Education,* XXIII, No. 3 (Fall, 1952), 34-48.

Friedlaender, Israel. "The Problem of Jewish Education in America and the Bureau of Education of the Jewish Community of New York City." *Report of the Commissioner of Education for the Year Ended June 30, 1913,* I, 365-93.

Gamoran, Emanuel, "Nationalism and Religion in Jewish Education," *Jewish Education,* VII, No. 1 (January-March, 1935).

Gartner, Lloyd P. "Rumania and America 1873: Leon Horowitz' Rumanian Tour and Its Background." *Publication of the American Jewish Historical Society,* XLV, No. 2 (December, 1955), 67-92.

———. "The Jews of New York's East Side, 1890-1893," *American Jewish Historical Quarterly,* New York: American Jewish Historical Society, 1964, Vol. LIII, No. 3 (March, 1964).

Handlin Oscar. "Judaism in the United States." *The Shaping of American Religion.* Edited by James Ward Smith and A. Leland Jamison. Princeton: Princeton University Press, 1961.

Herberg, Will. "Religion and Education in America." *Religious Perspectives in American Culture.* Edited by James Ward Smith and A. Leland Jamison. Princeton: Princeton University Press, 1961.

Higham, John. "Social Discrimination Against Jews in America, 1830-1930," reprinted from *Publication of the American Jewish Historical Society,* Vol. XLVII, No. 1 (Sept., 1957).

Honor, Leo L. "Jewish Elementary Education in the United States (1901-1950)." *Publication of the American Jewish Historical Society,* XLII, No. 1 (September, 1952), 1-42.

Huhner, Leon, "The Jews of New England (Other than Rhode Island) Prior to 1800," *Publications of the American Jewish Historical Society* (Baltimore: Lord Baltimore Press of The Friedenwald Company, 1903), Vol. XI.

Hutchinson, E. P. "The New Immigration," *The Annals of the American Academy of Political and Social Science,* CCCLXVII (September, 1966).

Jamison, A. Leland. "Religions on the Christian Perimeter." *The Shaping of American Religion.* Edited by James Ward Smith and A. Leland Jamison. Princeton: Princeton University Press, 1961.

Kaplan, Mordecai M. "The Meaning of Reconstructionism." *The Reconstructionist,* VI (February 16, 1940), 8-19.

Lifschutz, Ezekiel, "Yiddish Autobiographies as a Source of American Jewish History," *Publication of the American Jewish Historical Society,* Vol. LIII, No. 3 (March, 1964).

The New York Times, June 19, 1877.

Niebuhr, H. Richard. "The Protestant Movement and Democracy in the United States" *The Shaping of American Religion.* Edited by James Ward Smith and A. Leland Jamison. Princeton: Princeton University Press, 1961.

Philipson, David. "Letter to the Editor." *The American Israelite, December 28, 1899, 5.*
            . "Judaism in America." *The Universal Jewish Encyclopedia,* VI. Edited by Isaac Landman. New York: The Universal Jewish Encyclopedia, Inc., 1942, 240-43.

Prince, George M. "The Russian Jews in America," *Publication of the American Jewish Historical Society,* Vol. XLVII, No. 2 (December, 1958).

Rubenstein, Charles A. "The Reform Movement." *The Universal Jewish Encyclopedia,* III. Edited by Isaac Landman. New York: The Universal Jewish Encyclopedia, Inc., 1941. 101-103.

"Sabbath Schools," *Jewish Encyclopedia,* X. New York: Funk and Wagnalls, 1905. 602-603.

Siegel, Lawrence. "Reflections on Neo-Reform in the Central Conference of American Rabbis," *American Jewish Archives,* Vol. XX, No. 1 (April, 1968).

Tyack, David B. "The Perils of Pluralism: The Background of the Pierce Case." *The American Historical Review,* LXXIV, No. 1 (October, 1968), 74-98.

Weinryb, Bernard D. "The German Jewish Immigrants to America." *Jews from Germany in the United States.* Edited by Eric E. Hirshler. New York: Farrar, Straus and Cudahy, 1955, 103-26.

Wise, Isaac M. "Identity of the Mosaic State and the United States." *The American Israelite,* December 29, 1898, 4.

INDEX

A

Aboab, Isaac, 2
Addams, Jane, 67
Adler family, 27
Adler, Samuel, 35
Agricultural Colonies, 53, 54, 55
Aguilar, Moses, 2
Alabama, 28
Albany, New York, 3, 36
Alexander II, Czar, 47
Alexander, III, Czar, 60
Altman, Benjamin, 27
Amalgamated Clothing Workers Union, 58
American Christian Defenders, 78
American Communist Party, 78
American Israelite, The, 19
American Jewish Committee, 23, 25, 76
American Jewish Congress, 25, 26
American Jewish Joint Distribution Committee, 25
American Jewish Publication Society, 39
American Jewish Relief Committee, 25
American Legion, 74
American Protective League, 74
American Super-Race Foundation, 74
American Zion, 9
Americanization-definition, preface
Anti-Defamation League of B'nai B'rith, 24
Anti-Semitism, 2-4, 14-16, 20-23, 28-31, 34, 40-41(n. 21), 42(n. 47), 46-49, 76-79, 82
Arkansas, 10
Ash, Abraham Joseph, 67
Asiatic Exclusion League, 74
Astor, John Jacob, 6
Austria-Hungary, 15

B

Baker, Lafayette C., 29
Baltimore, Maryland, 28
Barbados, 2
Barsimson, Jacob, 2, 4
Beilis, Mendel, 48
Belkin, Samuel, 39
Belmont, August, 29

Benderly, Samson, 64, 65, 66
Benjamin, Judah Philip, 28-31
Berlin, Treaty of, 1878, 22
Berkowitz, Henry, 32
B'nai B'rith, 22, 24, 53
Board of Delegates of American Israelites, 25
Boaz, Franz, 79
Bolsheviks, 49
Bonaparte, Napoleon, 14, 15, 33
Boone, Daniel, 8
Borah, William, 61
Brandeis family, 27
Brandeis, Louis D., 58
Brazil, 2, 3
Browder, Earl, 78
Brownlow, William G., 29
Buchanan, James, 21, 22
Bund (Russia), 48
Bureau of Jewish Education, New York City, 63-66
Bush, Isidor, 28
Butler, Benjamin F., 29

C

Cahan, Abraham, 58, 59-61
Canada, 6, 7
Cantors, 5
Cap Makers Union, 58
Carigal, Haim Isaac, 5
Cass, Lewis, 21
Central Conference of American Rabbis, 32, 37, 82
Charleston, South Carolina, 5, 6, 18
Chaplains, Military, 29
Chicago, Illinois, 65
Chinese Exclusion Act, 74
Christian Century, The, 74
Church and State, 8, 9
Cincinnati, 28
Civil Rights Movement, 79
Cleveland, Grover, 74
Cohen, Jacob I., 8
Columbus Platform, See "Guiding Principles of Reform Judaism"
Communist Party, 60-61, 78
Conference of Presidents, 80

Congregations:
    Beth Elohim, Charleston, 32, 35
    Bene Israel, Cincinnati, 36
    B'nai Jeshurun, Cincinnati, 36
    Jeshuat Israel, Newport, 5, 11(n. 14)
    Bene Yeshurun, New York City, 38
    Beth Hamidrash Hagodol, New York City, 67
    Shearith Israel, New York City, 6, 11(n.14)
    Temple Emanuel, New York City, 67
    Mikveh Israel, Philadelphia, 6, 8, 11(n.14), 19, 32, 38, 39
    Rodeph Shalom, Philadelphia, 38
    Mickve Israel, Savannah, 7, 11(n. 14)
Cornell University, 78
Conservative Movement, 39, 84
Constitution, U.S., 8
Coughlin, Charles, 76
Cromwell, Oliver, 2
Cultural Pluralism, 79-80, 82
Curacao, 2
Cypress Bend, 10

D

Damascus Affaire, 20, 21, 25
Daughters of the American Revolution, 74
Dearborn Independent, 76
Defenders of the Christian Faith, 78
Dembitz family, 27
Der Tog, 51
Dewey, John, 79
Dietary Laws, 8, 40-41(n.21)
Dushkin, Alexander M., 63
Dutch, 2, 3
Dutch Reformed Church, 2
Dutch West India Company, 2, 3

E

Easton, Pennsylvania, 6
Economic Life, 3, 5-10, 26-28, 43(n.62), 49, 51, 52, 54, 55-59,
    78-79
Education, 14, 18, 31-33, 34, 47, 50-52, 62-67, 70-71(n. 45, 48,
    49, 55), 82
Educational Alliance, 67
Einhorn, David, 28, 35, 37
Einstein, Albert, 76
Einstein, Albert, Medical Center, 39

95

Elchanan, Rabbi Isaac, Theological Seminary, 39
Emanuel, David, 28
England, 2
Entertainment Industry, 81
Eugenics, 74

F

Fay, Theodore, 22
Federation Movement, 24, 80
Felsenthal, Bernard, 35
Ferdinand of Aragon, 2
Flexner family, 27
Florida, 28
Foote, Henry S., 30
Ford, Henry, 76
Forsyth, John, 21
Foster, William Z., 78
France, 14, 15
Franck, James, 76
Franco, Solomon, 2
Frankfort Assembly, 16, 17
Frankfurter family, 27
Franklin, Benjamin, 8
Franks family, 6
Frazier, E. Franklin, 79
Frederick William IV, 16, 17
Friedlaender, Israel, 66, 79
Fur Workers Union, 58

G

Galveston Plan, 53
Gamoran, Emanuel, 80, 82
Garment Industry, 56-59
Geiger, Abraham, 33
Georgia, 7, 8, 18, 28
German-American Bund, 78
Germany, 14, 15
Gimbel family, 27
Goldmark family, 27
Grand Island, 9
Grand Union Hotel, 31
Grant, Ulysses S., 22, 29, 31
Gratz College, 32
Gratz family, 6
Gratz, Rebecca, 38

Guadalupe, 2
"Guiding Principles of Reform Judaism," 82-83
Guggenheim family, 27

H

Ha-M'asef, 14
Hapgood, Hutchins, 63
Harby, Isaac, 18
Harding, Warren G., 74
Harkavy, Alexander, 59
Hart, Emanuel, 28
Hathaway, Clarence, 78
Hay, John, 19, 22
"Hebrews," 19, 20, 24
Hebrew Free Loan Society, New York City, 54
Hebrew Free School Association, 67
Hebrew Immigrant Aid Society, 54
Hebrew Institute, Chicago, 65
Hebrew language, 65, 83
Hebrew Sabbath School Union of America, 32
Hebrew Union College, 33, 37, 39
Heilprin, Michael, 28, 55
Henry Street Settlement, 67
Hillquit, Morris, 57
deHirsch, Baron Maurice, 54, 55
Hirsch, Samuel, 35, 36
Hitler, Adolph, 75
Holland, 2-4
Hoover, Herbert, 75
Hull House, 67
Hundt, Hartwig, 16

I

Immigration Restrictions, 74-76
Independent Order of B'rith Abraham, 54
Industrial Removal Office, 53
Inquisition, 2, 15
International Ladies' Garment Workers Union, 58
Isabella of Castille, 2
Isaacs, Isaiah, 8
Isaacs, Samuel M., 25, 28, 38
"Israel," 83, 86(n. 29)
Israel, State of, 76, 79, 80, 82
Israel's Herold, 28
"Israelites," 18, 19, 20, 43(n.66)

J

Jackson, Andrew, 9, 10
Jackson, Solomon, 19
Jacobs, George, 28
Jamaica, 2
The Jew, 16 (Germany), 19 (United States)
Jewish Agency (for Palestine), 25
Jewish Agricultural Society, 55
Jewish Alliance of America, 25
Jewish Chautauqua Society, 32
Jewish Colonization Association, 54, 55
Jewish Daily Forward, 58, 60
Jewish Theological Seminary of American, 33, 39, 66
Johnson, Andrew, 29
Johnson-Reed Immigration Act, 75
Joint Distribution Committee, 25
Joseph, Jacob, 68
Judaism-definition, preface

K

Kahn, Otto H., 27
Kalm, Peter, 6
Kallen, Horace, 79, 82
Kansas Post, 28
Kaplan, Mordecai M., 66, 79-80, 83-84
Kehillah, New York City, 65-66, 68, 71(n. 64)
Kentucky, 8, 9
Kerensky, Alexander, 49
Knights of Labor, 74
Kohler, Kaufmann, 37
Kotzebue, August von, 15
Kuhn, Loeb and Company, 27
Ku Klux Klan, 31, 74

L

Labor Unions, 56-59, 74
Lancaster, Pennsylvania, 6
Landsmanschaft, 54, 70(n. 26)
Lang, Harry, 61
Lazarus family, 27
Leeser, Isaac, 25, 29, 38, 39
Legardo, Elias, 2
Lenin, 49
deLeon, Daniel, 57
Lessing, Gotthold Ephraim, 14

Levin, Lewis Charles, 28
Levine, Morris, 65
Levy, Asser, 2
Levy family, 6
Levy, Hayman, 6
Levy, Uriah P., 30
Licking River, 8
Lilienthal, Max, 28, 35
Lincoln, Abraham, 29
Lindo, Moses, 6
Literary Societies, 24
Locke, John, 6
Loeb, Solomon, 27
Lopez, Aaron, 6
Loughlin, Harry, 74
Louisiana, 28
Louisiana Purchase, 9
Lumbrozo, Jacob, 7
deLyon, Abraham, 7

M

Madison, James, 9
Magnus, Judah L., 65, 66
Maimonides College, 39
Marshall, Louis, 58, 76
Martinique, 2
Maryland, 7
Massachusetts, 2
May Laws, 47, 48
Mendelssohn, Moses, 14, 33
Methodism, 7
Michelbacher, J. M., 28
Minhag Amerika, 36
Morais, Sabato, 19, 39
Mordecai, Alfred, 28
Mortara Case, 21, 25
Mortara, Edgar, 21
Mt. Sinai Hospital, New York City, 29
Myers, A.C., 29

N

Nathan the Wise, 14
National Council of Jewish Federations and Welfare Funds, 80
National Council of Jewish Women, 53
National Federation of Temple Sisterhoods, 67

National Hebrew Schools, 65
National Hebrew School for Girls, 65
National Jewish Community Relations Advisory Committee, 80
Nativist, 74, 77
Nazi, 78
Needle Trades, 56-59
Neumann, S. H., 65
New Amsterdam, 2-4
New Hampshire, 28
New Netherland, 2, 3
Newport, 5, 6, 9
New York City, 5, 6, 10, 28, 50
New York State, 8, 9, 28
Niagara River, 9
Nicholas I, Czar, 46
Nicholas II, Czar, 48
Noah, Mordecai Manuel, 9, 10, 28
Northwest Ordinance, 8

O

Occident, The, 39
Ochs, Adolph, 27
Oglethorpe, James, 7
Olat Tamid, 37
Order of '76, The, 78
Orthodox Movement, 36, 38, 39, 67-68

P

Pale of Settlement, 46
Park, Robert E., 79
Paul Reveres, 78
Peixotto, Benjamin Franklin, 22
Pennsylvania, 8, 28
Philadelphia, Pennsylvania, 5, 6, 9, 28
Philadelphia Conference (Reform), 36
Philanthropies, 24
Philips, Henry Myer, 28
Philips, Philip, 28
Philipson, David, 32
Pierce, Franklin, 22
Pinner, Moritz, 28
Pittsburgh Conference (Reform), 37
Pittsburgh Platform, 37, 38, 39
Pogroms, 47, 48
Poland, 46, 47

Politics, 48, 51
Politics-Office Holding, 6, 7, 9, 10, 28
Politics-Political Activity, 17, 18, 19
Portugal, 2
Poznanski, Gustav, 35
Press, Anglo-Jewish, 21, 39, 52, 81
Press, German language, 18, 20, 40(n. 12), 59, 81
Press, Hebrew language, 60
Press, Yiddish language, 51, 59-61, 81
Protocols of the Elders of Zion, 76

R

Rabbinical Assembly of America, 39
Rabbinical Council of America, 39
Rabbis, 5, 6, 34, 35
Raphall, Morris J., 28
Recife, 2
Reconstructionist Movement, 66, 83-84
Red Cross, 29
Reform Movement, 19, 31, 32, 33-38, 65, 82-83, 84
Reformed Society of Israelites (Charleston), 35
Revel, Bernard, 39
Revolutionary War, 7, 8
Rhode Island, 5, 6, 8, 9
Riesser, Gabriel, 16
Richmond, Virginia, 8, 28
Rivera, Jacob Rodriguez, 6
Roosevelt, Franklin D., 59, 60
Roosevelt, Theodore, 19, 23
Root, Elihu, 23
Rose, Ernestine, 28
Roumania, 22
Russia, 21, 22, 23, 25, 46-49
Russo-Japanese War, 48

S

Salomon, Haym, 7
Salvador, Francis, 6, 7
Sand, Karl Ludwig, 15
Saratoga Springs, New York, 31
Savannah, Georgia, 5, 7, 9
Schechter, Solomon, 39
Schiff, Jacob H., 27, 58
Seixas, Gershom Mendes, 6
Seixas, Moses, 8

Seligman family, 27
Seligman, Joseph, 29, 31
Selikowitch, George, 59
Settlement Houses, 54, 67
Sherman, William T., 31
Silver Shirts, 78
Smith, Al, 59
Smith, Gerald L. K., 76
Social Clubs, 24
Socialism, 48, 57, 58, 60, 61, 62
South Carolina, 6, 7, 18
Spain, 2
Stanley, Henry, 10
Statistics: Immigration and Population, 4, 7, 9, 10, 17, 20, 28,
    48-52, 70(n. 23), 75-76.
St. Charles, 2
Steffens, Lincoln, 60
Stiles, Ezra, 5
Straus family, 27
Straus, Isidor, 27
Straus, Nathan, 27
Straus, Oscar, 27
Supreme Council of Israelites, 14
Surinam, 2
Stuyvesant, Peter, 2-4
Swiss Treaty Affair, 21, 22
Switzerland, 21

T

Taft, William Howard, 23, 74
Tennessee, 9
Teutomania, 15, 16
Tauro, Isaac, 6
Triangle Shirt Waist Company, 58

U

Union of American Hebrew Congregations, 25, 32, 37, 53, 82
Union of Orthodox Jewish Congregations, 39
Union of Orthodox Rabbis, 39
Union Prayer Book, 37
United Hebrew Charities, New York City, 24, 53, 54
United Hebrew Trades, 57
United Jewish Appeal, 82
United Synogogue of America, 39
Untermeyer family, 27

V

VanBuren, Martin, 21
Vermont, 9
Versailles Conference, 1918, 25, 26
Vienna, Congress of, 15, 33, 34, 40(n. 5)
Virginia, 2, 8
Vorwartz, See; *Jewish Daily Forward*

W

Wald, Lillian D., 67
Warburg family, 27
Washington, George, 9
Wesley, John, 7
West Indies, 2
Wilson, Henry, 29
Wilson, Woodrow, 74
Wise, Isaac Mayer, 19, 20, 22, 25, 27, 28, 35, 36, 37, 42-43(n. 61),
    53
Wissenschaft des Judenthums, 33
World War I, 49
World Zionist Organization, 26

Y

Yeshiva University, 39
Yiddishe Gazetten, 60
Yiddish language, 50, 51, 57, 59, 61, 62, 65, 69(n. 17)
Yiddish Theatre, 61-62
Yiddishe Zeitung, 59
Young Germany Movement, 17
Young Men's Hebrew Association, 24, 66
Young Women's Hebrew Association, 66
Yulee, David Levy, 28

Z

Zionism, 25, 26, 32, 34, 35, 36, 37, 39, 43(n. 64), 65, 66, 81, 82,
    83
Zionist Organization of America, 82
Zunz, Leopold, 33